A TENPENNY DIP
IN PARADISE

A Tenpenny Dip in Paradise

Published by The Conrad Press Ltd. in the United Kingdom 2022

Tel: +44(0)1227 472 874
www.theconradpress.com
info@theconradpress.com

ISBN 978-1-914913-86-0

Printed and bound in Great Britain by Clays Ltd, Elcograf S.p.A

Typesetting and cover design by The Book Typesetters
www.thebooktypesetters.com

The Conrad Press logo was designed by Maria Priestley.

A TENPENNY DIP IN PARADISE

IN PARADISE

and other flights of fancy

Don Chapman

for my wife Sue

Contents

Preface

I n 1962 California University challenged Oxford University to an elephant race. A medical student called Raanan Gillon* picked up the challenge and came to the *Oxford Mail* for help. It was quite easy to find him an elephant, Bertram Mills Circus had one small enough to fly. Finding someone to transport it across the Atlantic was another matter. All the airlines declined, even Air India which had an elephant as its logo. The Air Ministry told me sniffily not to waste their time.

The United States Air Force was more sympathetic. Eventually I found myself talking on the hotline to the Commander in Chief of their forces in Europe. They had only one bomber big enough, but if it was going the right way at the right time, he assured me it would carry my elephant. For a few heady days I had visions of making history: becoming the first reporter to describe an intervarsity elephant race. Then the C-in-C rang me from Cologne, or was it Hamburg? Terribly sorry, the U.S. Pres-

* Now Emeritus Professor of Medical Ethics at Imperial College, London.

ident wouldn't allow him to compete with civil airlines.

The oddball story has always appealed to me. Since the age of seven when I made a primary school teacher laugh by ending a composition: 'Then the giant picked me up and blew his nose on me!' a wacky sense of humour sustained by a liking for treading the fine line between fact and fiction has underpinned a lot of my writing.

Looking back, I suppose the all-star variety bills my parents took me to at the New Theatre, Oxford, and the comedy shows we listened to on the radio helped fan a talent to amuse. Unlike the music hall comedians, I was no performer. As an Oxford University student, I took to writing about the theatre after I realised I was no good at acting or directing.

Reviewing plays as a graduate trainee reporter with the Westminster Press, first at Keighley, then Swindon, followed by thirty years as the *Oxford Mail* theatre critic, not only allowed me to satisfy a lifelong passion, to put into words the feelings and emotions I had witnessed on stage, it helped hone my skills as a descriptive writer, and that too affected my reporting. I became the journalist to turn to for tongue in cheek news reports and features.

Towards the end of 1964 Mark Barrington Ward, the second *Oxford Mail* editor I worked for, known in the office as BW, received a directive from London to brighten up the leader page, introduced the Anthony Wood Column, and invited me to write it. My namesake, the celebrated seventeenth century Oxford diarist and antiquary, Anthony à Wood, is said to have been a cantankerous individual, who did not suffer fools or people whose outlook he disagreed with gladly.

In contrast I adopted the buttonholing style that was becoming popular on radio and television. I made Anthony Wood a character who reflected the interests of my readers. Thanks to them I enthused about local history, the theatre organs that once rose out of the pit to entertain cinema audiences between films, giant pumpkins, allotments, horse trams, sunflowers, matchstick models, postcards, steam trains and other nostalgic flights of fancy.

After I took early retirement in 1994 a former colleague begged me to provide a weekly column for my local rag, the *Witney Gazette*: an opportunity to parade some of the absurdities from my life which had not appeared in print before.

The following selection, enhanced sometimes with photographs, occasionally with the cartoons of Jim Needle, an artist who shared my relish for the absurd, ranges the gamut from semi-serious to near bonkers.

1 – Growing up

A predigital childhood

In an age when children take television, i-phones, i-pads and i-pods for granted and have learnt to navigate the internet by the age of three this piece I wrote for the Oxford Mail Better Listening Supplement in 1961 – itself a misnomer in 2022! – recalls a technological world that has gone forever.

My early listening was confined to an old, upright wireless with a pile of dusty magazines on top, from which one wire (the aerial) disappeared crazily up to the picture rail, and another (the earth), frayed and bitten by generations of playful kittens, sank kinkily to a bracket on the cold-water pipe.

It survived my infant twiddling largely because, although I tried, I could not get the back off, and it had only three very solid knobs – off and on plus volume-control, a waveband switch and a huge programme-selector. The light no longer lit up the panel with its impressive list of stations. The glass, which protected it from fingers such as mine, was broken, and the pointer was bent, so that it was of no earthly use to the uninitiated.

In fact, when I fiddled with it, as I often did, I had to remember to return it to the particular spot in no-man's-land on the dial before I switched off, if I did not wish to incur the wrath of my father when he switched on again and – after the hum and crackle – some foreign voice spluttered over from outer space instead of the six o'clock news.

It was the first escape world I knew. On afternoons when the family was out, I would invite in the boy from next door – a more mundane spirit – climb up the back of the sofa and terrify him for hours on end by picking up messages from the dead, which had been floating around in the upper atmosphere for thousands of years, just waiting to shoot down our aerial, mutter a few words of gibberish into our loudspeaker, and slide gratefully to earth and a decent burial along our cold-water pipe.

Perhaps that is why to this day I am never comfortable in a room where there is a wireless without an earth. Sooner or later, I imagine, with all those sounds rushing around inside, screaming for release from limbo, it will – like Pandora's box – be broken open and a load of tormented spirits let loose.

Frustration at not being able to get the back off that old upright and settle its fate once and for all led me to experiment with other means of communication. At my insistence, I and the boy next door – who were never out of each other's sight except at bedtime – decided that we might have important thoughts to communicate to each other in the middle of the night, so we rigged up a couple of cocoa tins on a long lump of string. They never worked.

Nor did the set of ex-W.D. telephone equipment we bought with the proceeds of scrumping a neighbour's apple tree and selling the fruit up the road. Both were slung disgustedly into the attic. Instead, we fell to producing a magazine and hawking it around friends and neighbours at two-pence a read until, inevitably, the eleven-plus followed by a move of house, parted us for ever.

My parents bought a new wireless with preselected stations. About the same time I discovered crystal sets and became a genuine addict of the radio, staying awake under the bedclothes into the small hours listening to impossibly dull and incomprehensible talks and concerts. A one-valve set followed with its messy accumulator and I might have become a regular boffin but for a visit from my aunt.

My aunt left behind her a small, efficient wind-up gramophone and a pile of religious records ranging from a sermon by the Archbishop of Canterbury to the Salvation Army playing *Abide with Me*. My sister and I – the gramophone was nominally my sister's – soon tired of the doleful revivalist dirges, which were the main staple of our repertoire. But we got a lot of pleasure out of using our fingernails instead of the needle, and feeling the Archbishop's voice vibrating through our nervous systems like the trump of Armageddon.

Then a more frivolous lady of our acquaintance took pity on us and gave us an even larger pile of hits from the Twenties, so that I still sometimes surprise my friends by launching into some long-lost masterpiece like *When You Were the Girl on the Scooter and I Was the Boy upon the Bike, Oink, Oink!* Alas, the gramophone spring snapped one day when I was abusing the Archbishop and the house became silent except on those rare occasions when I could summon up the energy to turn the handle.

My interest in the wireless revived with the start of the Test Matches and soon I was sweating home from grammar school on my bike to glue my ear to those invisible commentators. During those dark days, when England's fight for the Ashes hung permanently in the balance, classes were intolerable and, as the headmaster refused to allow us to use the school radio – even in the lunch-hour – some means had to be found to keep us abreast of the titanic struggle.

An aerial was secreted behind the hot water pipes, a three-valve radio made specially for the purpose by a youthful technocrat was installed in his desk, and a wire ran from it inside his jacket, up his sleeve to a small earphone in his hand, upon which he rested his head in an attitude of casual boredom.

The master sat immediately in front of him on a dais behind a tall desk, upon the front of which he could chalk the scores minute by minute with complete impunity since, if the master chose to descend to the classroom floor to investigate the cause of our excitement, a quick flick of a duster removed all traces.

Looking back on it all now when we have an impressive seventeen-inch television set at home, my younger sister, Stella, has a small, immensely more efficient record-player, which refuses even to look at the Archbishop – he is so warped – and I can, if I wish, visit friends with expensive hi-fi equipment, which brings the sounds of a full orchestra into their drawing rooms, I realise that while I was twiddling, other more practical mortals were improving and inventing – and I must say – I am rather ashamed of my youthful flirtations with the medium of sound.

But the feeling of guilt never lasts long. Somewhere I like to think is a precocious seven-year-old sitting on a pile of books to get at the controls of his father's radiogram and twiddling – just as I used to do. He has heard of all those sad little satellites 'bleep-bleeping' away in space and, in particular, of that one the Russians have lost. What price the simple picture of delight on his face when that faint, tired, lost voice suddenly finds his aerial, utters a final, thankful 'bleep, bleep' into his loudspeaker, and sinks thankfully to earth along his cold-water pipe?

Oxford Mail 30 October 1961

Learning the chores

Like most children of our generation my sister Betty and I were expected to do our bit to help the smooth running of the Chapman household: pick grass for my father's rabbits, dry up for my mother, keep our bedrooms neat and tidy. But towards the end of the Second World War an accident occurred that transformed our domestic responsibilities.

A Queen Mary Lorry, one of those sixty-foot trailers that

transported broken aeroplanes to Cowley to be mended, clipped my mother off her bike and dragged her sixty yards along the road. For a week or two it seemed like touch and go whether she lived. For several months, despite her determination to return to running our Headington home, she was more or less an invalid, her arm in one of those frames then considered vital to the repair of badly broken bones.

My father was no cook. A boiling of potatoes and a mound of runner beans from the allotment was his idea of a feast. A tin of Spam or corned beef provided the protein, plus the occasional fried or hard-boiled egg. He was even less of a bottle washer. Doing the dishes was a chore. Scrubbing clothes and ironing them in the days before washing machines and drip-dry shirts was a mystery best left to the local laundry. Cleaning the home? He disliked household dirt as distinct from the good honest stuff he brought in from the garden, but he could never quite understand why my mother spent so much time on her knees polishing the floor or attacking every room with elbow grease and a duster.

As a result, at the age of eight, Betty effectively became housekeeper and I, aged ten, her general factotum. Armed with long shopping lists drawn up at my mother's dicta-tion, I would set off for Burrell's general store at the corner of Margaret Road. In my shopping basket – no disposable plastic bags in those days – I carried our ration books, which would be meticulously inspected on my return to make sure Burrell hadn't taken any coupons he ought not to have done, in my clenched fist a ten-shilling note. Woe betide me if I lost that – or the change!

With the aid of a wooden 'mushroom' I learnt to darn the holes that sprouted regularly in the toes and heels of my woollen socks. Some genius had yet to think of reinforcing them with man-made fibre. Patiently I would construct crossword grids of darning wool, fill them in with my needle, then offer them up for my mother's inspection. Why she made such a fuss about needlework that would be hidden under shoe leather I never understood, but fear of having to unpick them and do them again was sufficient incentive to make sure the lumpen patches passed muster.

I also must have cooked the occasional egg and panful of sausages, though curiously the only memories that survive are of peeling potatoes, shelling peas and trying to cut the crusty loaves the baker delivered to our door into neat slices without getting crumbs all over the kitchen floor, then spreading them with dripping. Butter was an occasional treat. It was rationed.

I probably learnt more by watching my sister preparing the meals under my mother's supervision than actually making such family favourites as steak and kidney pudding, shepherd's pie, toad-in-the-hole and dumpling stew myself. As a small boy it was amazing how much I took in by observation. Thirty years later when I came to paste up my first election-posters I realised to my surprise I knew exactly how to do it.

All that time I had wasted in my misspent youth gawping at billstickers proved worthwhile after all. The message I am trying to convey is that, unlike many of my contemporaries, I was house-trained. As a result of my mother's accident I became a thoroughly domesticated animal. In later life I have never ceased to be grateful for it.

At periods like the present, when my poor wife, Sue, is flat on her back with sciatica, I can take over the running of the household, even if she does need to remind me how to work the washing machine or take me to task for trying to bundle my smelly garden trousers in with her pants and vests. I do it all cheerfully with good grace. There are, though, enough of my father's genes in my makeup to prevent me finding it as rewarding as weeding my onion patch.

Only once have I experienced the rapturous satisfaction some people get out of housework. During my week's paternity leave after the birth of our elder daughter, Katie, I was walking along the landing one morning. I had just completed the complicated ritual nappy-washing involved in the days before disposables and happened to glance out of the window.

There they all were on the clothes line below, flapping in the breeze, whiter than white. For a moment I was lost in silent admiration of my handiwork. Then self-mockery reasserted itself. 'Silly old fool,' I chuckled to myself as I padded downstairs.

Witney Gazette 31 August 1995

Monday's washing day

The other day my wife bought a couple of rolls of film in Boots the Chemists. 'Don't you want your sandwich?' demanded the girl at the checkout counter. 'Sandwich?' said Sue. 'Yes, with every two rolls of Kodak colour film you're entitled to a free low calorie sandwich.'

I can see the logic of offering a free packet of Oxo cubes with a pound of minced beef, and I can appreciate why a waggish supermarket manager might give away a box of outsize gent's tissues with every two-kilo sack of Spanish onions, but films and sarnies? The connection escapes me. All the same, Boots sandwiches are good. Only a few days before we'd sat outside the Methodist Church munching our way through a packet while the traffic whizzed by in Witney High Street, so on this occasion Sue claimed her smoked ham and egg low calorie sandwich and we shared it for lunch.

In later life I have come to savour sarnies in every shape and form from banana mashed with demerara sugar in brown bread and butter to open top Danish extravaganzas supporting a mound of prawns or smoked salmon on a raft of crispbread. In my youth I loathed them.

Sandwiches meant cold meat from the Sunday joint stuffed between two slices of white bread with a smear of mustard, a dash of mint sauce or a dollop of stuffing. Monday was washday in our house and my mother hadn't got time to cook us lunch. No washing machines then.

By the time my sister and I came home from school at midday the operation would be well under way. The kitchen would be dripping with condensation from the gas-powered copper that heated the water. The washing would be ready to be lifted from its bubbling interior, rinsed in the sink, then fed through the mangle.

We turned the handle between mouthfuls, watching it squeeze out the moisture from the clothes we fed through the rotating rubber rollers. Then we dropped them in a tub for ma to hang out on the clothesline. If it wasn't raining, by the time we returned from afternoon school they would be dry enough to press.

The flat irons would be heating on the gas ring or by the fire in winter. Soon ma would be dashing away with the smoothing iron and my sister and I would be climbing the stairs to the bathroom with piles of neatly folded 'airing'. I can see ma still. She really did dash.

The smell of freshly laundered linen fills my nostrils again and I am reaching for the Daddies Sauce bottle to smother my supper. The dog looked forward to the bones, but rissoles made out of the last of the Sunday joint, minced up with onions and fried in flour with bubble and squeak containing the last of the Sunday veg ranked not much higher with us than cold meat sandwiches.

We preferred rabbit stew culled from the hundred or so prize-rabbits dad kept at the top of the garden – except when it involved killing one of our personal pets! – roast chicken, steak and kidney pudding, toad in the hole and curry the way an Indian missionary taught ma to make it with mashed potato and rice smothered in a thick white sauce.

By the time ma died she had learnt to punch the buttons

of an electronic washing machine with the best of them and I really looked forward to finding beef sandwiches in the vending machine at our office. Giving them away with films though? They will be offering a free set of prints next with every pack of processed cheese!

Witney Gazette 29 September 1994

The first of a series of occasional columns David Wynne-Jones, then editor of the West Oxfordshire weekly, twisted my arm to write after I took early retirement from the Oxford Mail in 1994.

Penny for a song

As my mother went about her housework in the 1930s and 1940s, she used to sing songs that must have been popular in her youth. I can see her now down on her knees polishing the floor to *My Blue Heaven*, the number with which Gracie Fields captured the hearts of the nation.

In her teens my sister, Betty, had a thing about a podgy, Brylcreemed singer called Guy Mitchell, who had a hit with a number called *Pretty Little Black-Eyed Susan*. She used to spend hours playing that record on her wind-up gramophone at the beginning of the 1950s. Goodness knows why, one stray line – 'I love my biscuits soaked in gravy' – refuses to erase itself from my memory.

I never caught the bug. Perhaps because I had two left feet and did not frequent the dance halls, perhaps because the chart-toppers of the pre-Beatles era were not as uplifting as the anthems I sang as a choirboy, I was never besotted with the ditties that came crackling over the radio.

I was hooked on the songs of the Victorian and Edwardian era. Another ex-choirboy, Chris Prior, and I formed a double act and used to sing them at St. Aldate's Church Youth Fellowship social evenings. In Market Street, Oxford, about where the drugstore is now, next door to Wenborn the Cutlers, a long-vanished emporium stuffed to the ceiling with knives, scissors and other deadly-looking implements, there was a music shop.

If I remember rightly, we went in search of the words and music for *Any Old Iron?* having failed to find them in the city's premier music shops, Taphouse's and Russell Acott's. For the equivalent of no more than 25p we came away with an armful of yellowing material, all still retailing at the prices it must have sold for before the First World War. The proprietor couldn't have had a clear-out since he set up in business.

Gathering dust behind the musical instruments, piano scores and dance band music most customers came in search of was a treasure trove of older melodies: *Where Did You Get That Hat? In the Twi-Twi-Twilight, The Good Ship Yacky-Hicky-Doolah, If It Wasn't for The Houses In Between, Boiled Beef and Carrots*. Though I dread to think how badly we sang them, we soon had a repertoire that would not have disgraced that doyen of the music hall, Harry Champion.

It wasn't enough to sing them. We had to have the props that went with them: the watch and chain that prompted the refrain: '*Any Old Iron?*' the pirate outfit for *The Good Ship Yacky-Hicky-Doolah*, the headgear to answer the question: 'Where did you get that tile? Where did you get that hat?' Somewhere along the line Chris decided a top hat wasn't good enough. He had to have one of those old-fashioned collapsible opera hats that folded flat when you sat on them and miraculously sprang open again when you shook them.

After drawing a blank at most of Oxford's outfitters, eventually we tried Hall Brothers, the university tailors in High Street. 'A collapsible silk opera hat?' said the elderly man behind the counter. 'It's years since anybody asked me for one of those. I'm not sure. I'll have to go and see.' A few minutes later he returned triumphantly from the stockroom, blowing the dust from a neatly folded parcel of tissue paper. 'There we are sir,' he said opening it.

It looked the sort of titfer that would cost a bomb. 'How much?' said Chris, fearing the silk masterpiece would be way beyond the reach of his schoolboy pocket. 'Let's see,' said the old man, inspecting the hand-written label tucked in the crown. 'Half-a-guinea. Ten-shillings-and-sixpence. Bless me, that's the price it must have retailed at before the war! But as nobody has thought to mark it up,' he added with a chuckle, 'and it's the last one I have, ten-shillings-and-sixpence it shall be.' For just over 50p Chris acquired a 'tile' that really did justify the refrain, *Where Did You Get That Hat?*

Witney Gazette 6 March 1996

My lightbulb moment

On one occasion our English master at the Oxford High School for Boys gave us 'The Man I Would Most Like to Have Been' as the subject of our weekly essay. For me it was a problem. I have never wanted to be anybody but myself. I went to the old City Library in St. Aldate's in search of inspiration.

Eventually, among the biographies of famous people, I stumbled on a life of Thomas Edison. I had no idea whether I would have liked to be the inventor of the electric light bulb. I'd never heard of him before. But he seemed the sort of chap who would be likely to appeal to my English master. I took the book home, regurgitated the juiciest bits over the weekend and on Monday handed in my essay.

The following week I found myself being held up as a shining example to the rest of the form. All my classmates had written glowing effusions about sportsmen, film stars, dance band leaders and the like. In my English master's eyes, I was the only boy who had upheld the honour of the human race.

Heaven knows what he would have said if we had been writing ten years later after Cliff Richard, Tommy Steele and the Beatles had burst upon the scene. He would probably have given us all a Wednesday detention and made us spend an afternoon when we should have been racing up and down the school playing field at Marston Ferry Road comparing one of Shakespeare's songs to the latest Rolling Stones hit.

He was like that. Though a life-long pacifist, who still wrote short, trenchant letters to the *Oxford Mail and Times* on the subject of nuclear disarmament, he took the same line as Nicholas Tate on heroes and heroines. In fact, it was the Government Chief Curriculum Adviser rapping modern teachers over the knuckles for not telling their pupils about British pin-ups like Alfred the Great, Nelson, Livingstone and Florence Nightingale that reminded me of F.W. 'Jock' Sutton and my essay on Edison.

I am not altogether in tune with Mr Tate's thinking. 'As a society we are sceptical about traditional heroes and heroines,' he told a Council of Europe conference in York, 'but tolerate the promotion among young people of celebrities from the world of pop culture, about whom a deeper scepticism would be in order.'

People like Oliver Cromwell and Sir Winston Churchill may have had a greater impact on our nation's history than the footballing legend, Sir Stanley Matthews, or the wartime Forces favourite, Dame Vera Lynn, but why shouldn't we revere them? Talk of King Henry VIII and you find yourself mentioning his wives as inevitably as speaking of Michael Jackson you think a little dubiously of his friendships with children.

In the past when people relied on word of mouth no doubt old codgers in Bampton held village lads spellbound with stories of how they and the Duke of Wellington bashed Old Boney at the Battle of Waterloo. In Ascott-under-Wychwood, I am sure parents handed down to their children just as vivid tales of how sixteen village women went to prison in 1873 for supporting a strike by their farm labourer husbands and sons for an extra two bob a week.

I have never been a pop music fan. I couldn't name a single hit of Blur or Oasis. I manage to watch quite a lot of sport on the box without being able to remember more than a handful of names of the leading participants. Even my worship of the great actors and actresses who have made such a difference to my life falls well this side of idolatry.

In an age when the news media allow us to see so much of what is going on around the world at close quarters and expose the slightest fall from grace to public gaze, it is very difficult to believe in and look up to the sort of heroes and heroines Mr Tate would like us to. For every blue-rinsed lady or blue-blazered gentleman who thought Mrs Thatcher was wonderful, there were others who reached for the off button at the mere mention of her name.

She has her place in history and no doubt one day, like Boadicea, will also have a place in our school history books. As Gordon Marsden, the editor of *History Today*, points out: 'You cannot have history without being taught about great figures,' but he is careful to add: 'nor without ordinary people.'

Witney Gazette 28 October 1995

A bit off the top

Like the majority of men in West Oxfordshire I suspect, I go to a unisex salon these days when I want a haircut. Not very often. I hate parting with any portion of my anatomy from my topknot to my toenails. More to the point, my wife, Sue, who makes my appointments and briefs the hairdresser, prefers my hair long.

At first it was rather disconcerting to sit next to Mrs X while she slowly frizzed under a great plastic bonnet or rub shoulders with Mrs Y while expert hands restored the colour to her hair with an evil-smelling purple dye. I objected to young ladies asking me brightly between scissor-snips was I going anywhere nice at the weekend? – the last thing I wanted was to hit the town after working all hours as a journalist.

Gradually I succumbed to the rituals of the perfumed temple. The handmaiden with the expensive ash-blonde coiffure, who sighed over my silver locks: 'I wish I had hair that colour,' softened me up. Melanie completed my seduction. She is the wife of one of the village builders and daughter of another well-known Eynsham resident. We share common interests. In the few minutes it takes her to tidy my unruly thatch we can hold an intelligent conversation. I emerge feeling well-groomed, like a dog or a horse, not the shorn lamb who crept home from the barbers of my youth.

What prompted these tonsorial musings was the sudden realisation that the hairstyle most young men under a certain age seem to sport at the moment is – granted a bit more on top – the same pudding basin cut that prevailed when I was a boy. Short of shaving your head – which meant you had nits – the aim was to crop your hair as close to your scalp as possible to delay forking out another shilling for as long as you could.

The expression 'short back and sides' meant what it said. A barber in Headington attacking my hair with too much vigour once nicked my ear with his scissors. They ran their hand-clippers up the back of your neck as if they were mowing an overgrown hayfield. They scraped away your sideboards with a cutthroat razor. There was no finesse about the service or the establishment.

A dollop of hair cream or a quick squirt of scented water that hit your head like a minor cloudburst. A few tugs with a comb and thumps with a brush, then it was: 'Next please.' Bottoms shuffled along the wooden bench, edging closer to the one well-thumbed copy of the day's paper and, provided some old cock didn't want the full works – shave, haircut and shampoo – in a few minutes it was your turn. Nobody made an appointment. Nobody thought of their barber as a hair stylist.

It wasn't until I became choirboy at St. Aldate's Church in Oxford and took to having my hair cut in the hour between school and choir practice I stumbled on an elderly barber in the back streets who clearly was, or had been, a tonsorial artist. A great circle of scissors, razors and clippers adorned one wall. An array of diplomas and gold medals won in Paris in the 1890s festooned another. He snipped away in silence and I was too young, too awestruck, to break it. But oh, what questions I would ask if I could turn back the clock!

Witney Gazette 10 November 1994

Cardboard milk-tops

The milkman making his deliveries with a chorus line of dancing milk bottles is one of my favourite television commercials at the moment. It appeals to my sense of the ridiculous to think the empty I put outside my front door last thing at night has a life of its own before it reappears silver-hatted and semi-skimmed first thing in the morning. The reality, of course, is rather different. The environmentally friendly glass bottle has been losing ground to the cardboard carton for several years and now the plastic container is shoving the carton off the supermarket shelves.

I arrived in the world a few years too late to remember the milkman who went from door-to-door ladling milk from the churns he carried on his pushcart into the customer's own jug. By the time I was old enough to take an interest the broad-necked glass bottle was ubiquitous with its circular waxed cardboard lid. The device was a good deal more user-friendly than the buttoned-down ears of the cardboard cartons which defy your best efforts to turn them into spouts without spilling half the contents on the floor.

The circular cardboard milk-top had at its centre a smaller circle, which gave way to the pressure of your thumb, allowing you to slip your finger into the resulting hole and lever off the lid. Occasionally the bottling machine would insert two lids in the neck by mistake or the centre would fail to respond to pressure resulting in a squirt of liquid across the breakfast table. Usually, it did its job without fuss and my juvenile attention focussed on what happened to the lid after the milk bottle was empty. Not only did the underside attract a thick layer of cream to lick off, the cardboard disc itself was a prize.

Like other small girls and boys, my sister and I collected cardboard milk-tops. The gaily coloured slogans the different dairies printed on them gave them the same sort of appeal as cigarette cards and postage stamps. The best ones, preferably with the centres still intact, we kept in a box. The seconds we took to school and swapped or used to play a game that for a while was as popular as conkers. Placing the disc between your index and middle fingers, you flicked it like a Frisbee against the wall and, if you succeeded in landing on your opponent's milk-top, you claimed them both.

No doubt my collection would have some curiosity value now, but an eight-year-old boy has no thought for posterity. I probably swapped it for a handful of marbles or a tyre for one of my Dinky toys. In due course the narrow-necked bottle with its metal foil cap made the wide-necked bottle with its cardboard lid obsolete. A few decades later came cardboard cartons and now plastic containers are muscling in on the act.

Muscling is the right word. Undoing their plastic screw caps is not a job for weak fingers. I retain my allegiance to the glass bottle. The very thought of my friendly neighbourhood milkman playing Pied Piper to a chorus line of plastic containers fills me with alarm. It would sound like a herd of cows in wellington boots!

Witney Gazette 8 June 1995

Woolly pompoms

Several readers have pointed out that I failed to mention the most important after-use of cardboard milk-tops: making woolly pompoms. It must have been a Freudian slip. Having licked the cream from the underside of the lid and washed it carefully to remove all traces of grease, you removed the perforated centrepiece. Then you settled down with the resulting cardboard O, preferably two Os back-to-back to provide a firmer framework, and a skein of wool.

You wound the wool around the milk-top working in a clockwise direction until it was so fat you couldn't poke the end through the centre even with a darning needle. Then you snipped carefully around the circumference with a sharp pair of scissors, tied the strands firmly at the middle and – hey presto! – you'd made yourself a wonderful, perfectly spherical woolly pompom. In the days before Blue Peter on television it was the sort of useful tip on what to do with discarded materials you found in comics like the *Dandy* and *Beano*, *Wizard* and *Hotspur*.

Another, I remember, was making table mats with four small nails and a wooden cotton reel. You half-hammered the nails in square formation into one end of the cotton reel. Then you wound wool round them. By lifting the woollen loops over the heads of the nails you produced a thin woolly sausage, which dangled down the shaft of the cotton reel. If you kept going long enough – I never did! – you eventually had enough sausage to coil up like a snake and stitch into a place mat.

More popular with boys growing up during the Second World War was using the same wooden cotton reels, rubber bands, matchsticks and drawing pins to make tanks. By nicking notches in the rims of the cotton reels you could make your tank with its elastic motor climb small obstructions like fingers and pencils.

Miss expected us all to do our bit for the war effort in my class at Margaret Road Junior School, Headington. Those boys and girls who could knit made khaki, navy and Air Force blue scarves for our freezing soldiers, sailors and airmen. Those like me she couldn't trust to produce string dishcloths with outsize needles without dropping stitches made woolly pompoms.

She gave us a big cardboard O the size of a tea plate, a pile of tangled wool and told us to get on with it. The wool in my pile wasn't just tangled. It was tied in the most excruciating knots. While other Os waxed fat as full moons as the weeks went by, mine remained as lean as the kine in the Bible. I can hear Miss now: 'Come along, Donald, stop daydreaming and start winding. By the time you've finished the war will be over!'

Eventually I took to winding chunks of knotted wool into my O, then jumping on it when Miss wasn't looking to try to flatten out the lumps. By the time the more nimble-fingered of my classmates had finished I realised the dreadful implications of what I had been doing. If and when Miss cut open my pompom it would fall apart.

The 1944 equivalent of the eleven-plus saved me. I won a scholarship to Oxford Boys High School, handed in my unfinished lumpen O and left. By comparison grappling with Latin conjugations and declensions was a doddle.

I have often wondered since what happened when the poor, unsuspecting pupil who inherited it took it to Miss to have it cut open. I have also wondered what contribution all those pompoms made to the war effort.

Did girls in bomb factories use them as padding to prevent their deadly products exploding before they reached their destination? Were they some sort of psychological weapon? Fritz, cowering in his trench, would hear the Allied bombers droning overhead, the whistle of dropping incendiaries, then – pat! – a soft woolly pompom would strike him on the end of his nose.

As he worried if the pompom was impregnated with some deadly nerve agent his mate, staring at my woolly pompom, hanging like a splattered plate of spaghetti from his helmet, would drop dead with shock on the spot!

Witney Gazette 29 June 1995

Our golden yesterdays

The other day I was reading a review of a new book by Joan Evans called *The Victorians* when I came across the quotation: 'Any sensible Englishman of the upper or middle class might wish that he had been born in the spring of 1834 and died in the spring of 1914 at the age of eighty.' And why? Apparently, that was 'the latest time when he would have had real continuity of life and have been warmed by a steady belief in progress'.

But is that what we want, upper, middle or lower class, from our four score years on earth? In a review of another book, Anthony Birley's biography of *Marcus Aurelius*, that worthy Fellow of All Souls, Dr A.L. Rowse, takes care to point out that it was from the blissful security of the eighteenth century that Gibbon penned his famous dictum: 'If a man were called to fix the period in the history of the world during which the condition of the human race was most happy and prosperous, he would without hesitation name that which elapsed from the death of Domitian to the accession of Commodus.'

Today we have the benefit of modern scholarship and know that the Rule of the Five Good Emperors was not such a bed of roses. Today we have the benefit of living in the twentieth century, and don't let's underestimate it.

When I was a teenager lying on the operating table at the Radcliffe Infirmary having my lip stitched up after running into the back of a coal lorry on my bicycle at dusk, it struck me forcibly. How terrible it would have been if a Norman axe had sliced a lump out of my face at the Battle of Hastings in 1066. Without anaesthetics and a skilful surgeon with a needle and some catgut I would probably have got gangrene and become a gibbering idiot. Harold was lucky he got an eyeful not a mouthful.

We don't normally consider the physical shortcomings of living in the past. That wouldn't be fair. Otherwise, historians would always be writing silly footnotes like: 'Not having studied domestic science at school, Nell Gwynne didn't mind who fingered her oranges.'

No, we regard past, present and future with a spirit of

adventure and I for one am alarmed that Dr Evans should plump for an era in memory of whose Queen she dressed her dolls in black as a child. Without hesitation I would have chosen the first Elizabethan Age when it was all happening: the sailors making their voyages of discovery around the world, the scientists hoping to turn lead into gold, the English language teeming with a wealth of new found words.

Or, if my time machine would only carry me forward, I would have settled as readily for the second Elizabethan Age when, trusting our Queen lives to 2022, the pulse of adventure will have quickened again to meet the challenge of a brave new universe.

Despite the fact that in the last fifty years we have made more progress than in the previous 500, our own era is too introspective. We are as afraid of death and damnation as they were in the Middle Ages. The nuclear age has robbed us of our self-confidence. Poets scribble private thoughts on the peeling walls of their souls. The new image-makers whir their cameras to the sound of music or probe the meaningless junk shops of everyday life. The new word makers are the technologists, unscientifically screwing Latin nuts onto Greek bolts.

What everybody needs is a booster rocket for their ego, tangible proof that the sky is not the limit, evidence that there are another hundred unknown worlds and, when they get it, I believe humanity will bubble over again with excitement as Albion did in the sixteenth century, as Athens did in the time of Pericles, as Rome did in the time of Julius Caesar. The last age when an Englishman of the upper or middle classes had real continuity of life and was warmed by a steady belief in progress indeed! You would think everybody had already gone to the moon – and nobody had come back.

Oxford Mail 27 August 1966

2 – University

My ambition when I left the Oxford High School for Boys in 1949 was to become a solicitor. The head of the firm I consulted told me I would have to pay a premium of £300 to become articled to him and I could not expect to earn enough to support myself until near the end of the five-year indenture period. No problem, I thought. While I'm doing my National Service I'll save up.

That fond dream evaporated when the military authorities classed me Grade III and rejected me because I was underweight for my height. Instead, I became a junior book clerk at Oxford University's Bodleian Library. Worried I suppose that I might collapse under an armful of priceless manuscripts they sent me for a medical to their own consultant in St. Giles. He told me to strip off, turned round, took one look at me and asked: 'Young man, how do you expect to get through life with a body like that?' He could find nothing wrong with me though so the library kept me.

It had an arrangement whereby junior staff could read for a pass degree in their spare time. After a year I applied and was sent for an interview with the Revd. V. J. K.

Brook, the Censor of St. Catherine's Society, at what is now the Music Faculty in St. Aldate's. After a few routine questions, he said: 'See you in October.' It was a formality – the library was paying my fees and had given me its blessing.

In the sixth form I had studied Greek and Latin. The Society had no classics tutors. They farmed me out to the University Public Orator and Fellow of Jesus, J. G. Griffith. He was to change the course of my life. Sharing my love for translation, he took a shine to me. When I passed classical prelims after two terms he said: 'You're wasting your time, Don. You would have no problem gaining a county major award. You should come up full time and read for an honours degree.'

Passing what was to all intents and purposes an exam for sportsmen and students with other priorities precluded me from tackling Classical Moderations and I did not fancy the history and philosophy of Greats. 'What about Oriental Languages?' he said.

I got hold of a copy of the University Gazette. There were five or six students reading Sanskrit, fewer reading Arabic and the other languages on offer and fewer jobs still when they graduated, so I opted to study English Literature. The library was not pleased and made sure nobody followed my example.

Chesney Horwood, the Dean of St. Cat's, liked to tutor every English intake himself, but because I switched had to farm me out for my first term to Freddie Bateson at Corpus Christi College. Although I didn't recognise it at the time, the editor of the scholarly journal, Essays in Criticism, was to influence the course of my life too.

'Poor chap,' I thought. 'He's got to listen to all these essays every week on Shakespeare's comedies, tragedies, histories and problem plays. I'd better write interesting essays or he's not going to be interested in me.' Six weeks in he said to me: 'You write lively essays. You should be a journalist!'

Like a lot of my contemporaries, I had given no thought to what I might do after I graduated. Suddenly, as I was about to enter my final year, I recalled what he had said and thought I'd better produce some stories to show employers.

By chance a St. Cat's man, Tony Jaffé, had just been appointed to edit the student newspaper, Cherwell. 'Sure, Don,' he said, 'write me a few pieces in the long vac.' I wrote five and all five were printed in the first issue. Nobody else had bothered. In the next two terms before I focussed on my finals I produced a steady stream of stories, articles and editorials.

The university was a far more chauvinist institution than it is today. The women's colleges – there were no mixed colleges then – kept their students in virtual purdah. A man could not visit a woman's room without a chaperone. There was even a club with a dark blue tie and a gold bath tap for men who managed to bath in a women's college. They had to bring back the tap top to prove it!

I wrote the following editorial when two gowned Proctors and a team of bowler-hatted assistants known as Bulldogs, policed student activity like visiting out of bounds bars or being out after midnight. The Proctor would stop you, doff his mortarboard, and ask politely: 'Excuse me, sir, but are you a member of this university?' If you were, you were honour bound to reply yes.

Suddenly in Michaelmas Term 1955, the police started stopping students they suspected of infringing university rules and passing their names to the Proctors. The story made national headlines and provoked outrage among past and present students. Nobody questioned the logic of the midnight curfew. It was the civil police usurping the university police's powers that upset everybody.

Narked

… well, as I was saying, there was me an' there was Lulu – he's only 'alf sharp – but he 'andles a safe like it wuz 'is woman, and there wuz Marlene – first time I used a dumb on a job – she 'eld the torch… now Lulu pops the twiddler an' is just scooping the ready into my briefcase when in breezes some swell bonanzer in a blackout curtain, lifts 'is breadboard an' sez: 'Hexcuse me, gentlemen, but would you be hevading the hatttention of my colleagues, the civil custodians of the peace?' – you know, smug, pie, a crack on 'is dial like the slice of a melon – well, o' course, this sends ole Lulu round the bend an' I aint quite on board either… but Marlene, smart broad, Marlene, catches a snifter and starts giving the green light, fast, to one of his stools in a bowler 'at… didn't bat an eyelid, completely in'uman… so she tries the other one – no go, must uv 'ad their mouths

41

stuffed – meantime big boy's givin' the scraperboard treatment to Lulu... and Lulu gets scared... then 'e mentions the rozzers – that did it – Lulu dropped 'im cold – the bowler-'atted boys?... huh, they scarpered like dey wuz lambs – I tell you, it beats me – what did they think we were, anyway? – college boys?

Cherwell 29 November 1955

3 – Trainee journalist: Keighley

Jobs in journalism are now like gold dust. There were not many in 1956. With the help of the University Careers service I identified four possibilities. Three fell through. The fourth was a graduate traineeship with Westminster Press. The Group training officer, Philip Duncum, interviewed me at the Oxford Mail and Times offices in New Inn Hall Street where I would later work. There were thirty-three applicants for two posts and I was lucky enough to get one of them. You spent eighteen months learning your trade at one of the group's weeklies followed by eighteen at one of its dailies. My weekly was the Keighley News in West Yorkshire, my daily the Swindon Evening Advertiser.

Joey, my first scoop

My wife, Sue, popped into Dovecote, the pet store in Witney High Street the other day to have a word with the guinea pigs at the back of the shop. 'Hello,' a voice greeted her. 'Hello,' she replied. 'How are you?' the voice continued. 'I'm all right,' she responded. 'How are you?' 'You do talk well,' her newly acquired feathered friend informed her. Mickey the mynah bird was indulging in his favourite pastime: chatting up the customers.

I've interviewed quite a few talking birds in my long career as a journalist from dyslexic budgies to blasphemous parakeets. Former colleagues still recall with mirth how I came back from the talking bird contest at the National Cage Bird Show in Birmingham with a mild dose of psittacosis: parrots' disease. But the one that sticks in my mind is Joey.

Early in my first eighteen months as a trainee reporter at Keighley Charlie Senior thrust an advertisement under my nose one Friday morning. 'Lost,' it said. 'Blue and white budgerigar. Can say its own name and address.' 'See if there's anything in it, lad,' the veteran news editor said. I wasn't that keen. Talking budgerigars are not that unusual. It was my long weekend off. By the time I'd called on the owners and written the story, if there was a story, I'd probably have missed the midday train back to Oxford.

'No,' insisted Charlie, 'You go, lad. I've got a feeling.' 'He was right. Joey turned out to belong to a seriously disabled eleven-year-old girl. Not realising the budgie's cage was open, the girl's mother had opened the living room window and the bird had sped off into the wide blue yonder.

The poor woman and her husband were distraught. Joey was not just another pet budgerigar who could say his own name and address. He was his young owner's only means of expression. He could recite the name and address and all the nursery rhymes she was unable to repeat herself. 'If Belinda comes back from hospital and Joey is not here to

44

greet her the bottom will drop out of her world,' her mum told me. 'That bird means everything to her.'

I went back to the office, wrote my story, phoned it over to our sister evening newspaper in Bradford, the *Telegraph and Argus*, caught my train, and returned on Monday morning to find Joey had become the talk of West Yorkshire.

An old man had nearly got run over by a bus trying to capture an escaped budgerigar with his hat. A woman had driven all the way from Leeds with her reluctant, tearful daughter in case her newly acquired pet was the missing Joey. A pile of messages on my desk bore testimony to the fact that the Reporters Room telephone had hardly stopped ringing throughout the weekend.

The errant bird was already home. Farfetched as it sounds, he had caught a claw in the boot scraper outside a pet shop a few yards from the *Keighley News* office and the pet shop owner had rescued him. I set off to interview him.

Every window in the house was firmly shut, but his cage door was open and within seconds of me entering the room an unbelievably bedraggled budgerigar was on my shoulder. He told me his name was Joey. He correctly gave me his address. Then he launched into a seemingly endless repertoire of nursery rhymes.

He never said a word about his adventure, nor back at the office did Charlie remind me how close I had come to missing my first scoop. Punching me on the shoulder in his usual affectionate way, he said: 'Cracking yarn! Well done, lad.'

Witney Gazette 27 April 1995

Exit the gas lamp

Exit the Victorian gas-powered streetlamp. Enter the electricity man with his unadorned standard of precast concrete and his amber-coloured lantern. Paddington may protest. The cartoonist, Ronald Searle, may lament with his pencil the departure of his beloved bric-a-brac to people tram-strewn graveyards with Victorian lampposts, but not Keighley. In Devonshire Street the gas lamps are coming down and the electricity standards are going up with never a murmur.

This week a *Keighley News* reporter, making a light-hearted inquiry into the inhabitants' views on the scene change, occasioned only surprise, and ruffled one or two stern business men, concerned after their lunches with weightier matters. 'I hadn't really noticed,' said a housewife, still wiping the washing-up water from her hands. 'I suppose they were beautiful,' pondered an old lady. 'We must move with the times, you know,' chuckled a friendly solicitor, and winked conspiratorially as if he had uncovered a plot for a revolution against the Council. Outside a dog sniffed suspiciously at the new concrete, and preferred the familiar green paint.

Mr Reynolds of the North Eastern Gas Board said the gas lamps had been there at least fifty years – as long as he has been with the gas industry – and probably longer. They originally had the ordinary lantern-shaped heads, but just before the last war they were given their present graceful necks and pleasant dewdrop type lamps.

Why are they going? With all due reverence to these

46

ancient ladies of the street they had become too old. They were uneconomical and their light did not shine brightly enough. The electric standard had outclassed them both in cheapness and efficiency.

Yet we suspected a few old-fashioned sentimentalists like ourselves would shed the metaphoric tear and make a last visit to hear the swansong of these delicate creatures that swam in their own small pools of wavering gaslight, hissed proudly at passers-by, arching their slender necks in the darkness, and sometimes… just sometimes… went 'pop' in the night.

I wrote this piece for the Keighley News, probably in 1957. Sadly, the clipping I kept is not dated. At the time councils all over the country were provoking outrage among conservation groups by switching from gas to electricity and scrapping old-fashioned street lamps for concrete standards. The cartoonist Ronald Searle had a field day.

Mucking the pigs out and other mischief

When I entered journalism, it was the job of junior reporters to read the galley proofs, the equivalent, I suppose, in those hot metal days, of the computer print-out of today. Woe betide the lot of us if we failed to spot an error and it appeared in next Saturday's *Keighley News*.

I mention the fact not because of the number of misprints that now disfigure the most prestigious books and journals, though it does strike me the whole publishing world could benefit from a small army of juniors to monitor the daily output on their computer screens. No. It was the way certain stories turned up among the galley proofs week after week that suddenly tickled my memory apropos of nothing the other day.

In particular I remember a long slab of type headed New Developments in Pig Farming by Our Agricultural Correspondent. Being a West Yorkshire mill town, Keighley didn't go much on pigs or farming. In fact, it hadn't had an agricultural show since 1906 when an intrepid lady parachutist, hired no doubt at great expense to enliven the proceedings, became detached from her skyhooks as she jumped from a balloon and plunged to her death.

Consequently, if there was a surfeit of news when the paper was 'put to bed' at Bradford on Friday, which there usually was, the editor would say to the printers: 'Better hold the pigs for next week.'

The galley proofs were produced by running an inky roller over the slabs of type, then taking impressions from them with another dry roller on damp strips of paper. After a few weeks ink on the typeface became clogged, the galley proof became illegible and the junior, whose lot it was to read it, would take it to the News Editor.

'Time to muck out the pigs again, is it, lad?' Charlie Senior would say. He liked his little joke. A note would be dispatched to Bradford by the afternoon van. Some poor printer's devil would clean up the typeface. Next morning a pristine galley proof would arrive and one of us would settle down to read New Developments in Pig Farming for the umpteenth time.

The article no doubt found its way into the paper during Wakes Weeks, the fortnight when all the textile mills closed down and half the town's population departed on holiday. Once we'd chronicled the mass exodus – 'Bognor Challenges Blackpool as Most Popular Destination' – it was difficult for even the more imaginative and inventive of us to find enough material to fill the slimmed down edition minus most of its regular advertisements that appeared those two weeks.

But when things returned to normal, inevitably there would be some piece of deathless prose to take the place of New Developments in Pig Farming among the galley proofs. Mercifully I cannot recall an article of mine suffering that fate, though probably more than one did.

But I do remember that it was the author of New Developments in Pig Farming who, inadvertently, might have got me the sack. The only indication that the paper's most senior reporter was also its agricultural correspondent was a pair of wellington boots he kept under his desk. He never wore them. They served as a receptacle for his empty beer bottles.

Having nothing better to do one Friday afternoon, I emptied them, tied them to a piece of string and dangled them out of the third floor Reporters' Room so the toes just tapped the window of the Advertising Department below. At that moment the Advertising Manager's secretary looked up, saw what she thought was someone about to plunge to their death like the lady parachutist and fainted at her boss's feet.

It was not the only prank of mine that might have earned me my notice. Another senior reporter specialised in compiling the trade pages in support of full- or half-page advertisements promoting new products. It was his practice to stop typing at 12.30pm, go home for lunch, then resume typing without bothering to re-read his copy.

One day he left in the middle of writing a piece about a new car that has just come on the market. In his absence I added the sentence: 'In order to enhance the luxuries of the new model the manufacturers have dispensed with the engine under the bonnet and installed a refrigerator.'

He came back, finished the piece and dropped it in the copy basket. Charlie Senior picked it out, read it, came up to my desk, waved it under my nose with a huge grin, punched me on the shoulder and said: 'Yer bugger!'

Witney Gazette 20 March 1996

A tenpenny dip in paradise

The first time I had a public bath was after the landlord took the tops off both bath taps. Until then I had managed by unscrewing the top off the cold water tap and screwing it onto the hot one. I must admit it relieved my conscience.

As October gives way to November even the least suspicious of canny Yorkshiremen will find it hard to believe that the thin-blooded Southerner, who slips out of his front door every morning in scarf and overcoat, really enjoys a cold bath. Anyway, chasing steam through the fanlight and scrupulously wiping the condensation from the tiles had grown tiresome, not to mention that the men had been three times to inspect the back boiler that didn't seem to be working properly.

So, on the friendly advice of the landlord – God rest his soul in hot water somewhere! – I went to the Municipal Baths down the road, a large towel wrapped round a change of underclothing, my soap in a little plastic box and a scrubbing brush in my pocket.

I was apprehensive and I had put it off as long as I could; in fact, until the fear of exposing myself in public at all and the shame of exposing myself in a state any grubbier had reached equilibrium.

The notice on the door, which read: 'Women: Mondays, Wednesdays and Fridays. Men: Tuesdays, Thursdays and Saturdays', removed one doubt, and the question of the cashier dispelled another. 'Do you want a plain slipper bath or do you want a first class one?' she inquired.

I have always travelled second class on public transport, but in public baths – as I realised at once – I was more particular. Ideas of baths without plugs, tin baths, baths in a communal bathhouse on rubber mats vanished rapidly down the plugholes of the plain slipper baths. 'A first class one,' I said. 'That will be tenpence, please,' she replied.

'Towel? Soap? Bath salts?' What could I say? I had brought my own towel and soap and I had never used bath salts since my cousin presented me with a jar she had made at home from common soda and coloured inks. But how would the cashier think I could wash myself without soap, how dry myself without a towel, how soften the hardness of those Pennine waters without bath salts?

I handed over one and fivepence for a tenpenny bath, a fourpenny towel, a twopenny tablet of soap and a penny bath cube, and went and joined a queue of grey men on a wooden bench. At intervals a whistle blew, the man nearest jumped up, a door opened, a cloud of steam and light burst forth, and he vanished into the heated abyss. The bottoms slid along the bench. No one came out.

I suppose it was the mystery of this that made me slide automatically onto the floor when the whistle blew for me. But I picked myself and made the plunge. And, oh the folly of ignorant prejudice, I issued into paradise. Angelic voices rose from nowhere, water splashed happily to the tune of celestial laving, and a cherubic little man motioned me to a spotless closet, wherein stood the largest bath I had ever seen, filled to the brim with piping hot water, a heavenly loofah floating on its surface.

Much later I emerged in that blissful euphoria a well-taken bath evokes, pressed sixpence into his hand and passed through another door into the night. It was then I discovered bathing in public has its drawbacks. Beads of perspiration formed on my face. A chill wind made the gas lamps flicker. And I realised I should catch a cold every time I performed this ritual pleasure.

I rushed to the nearest cinema to dry out. Pondering on the capaciousness of public baths now, when I lie soaking at home in Oxford, my lean length folded into much shorter dimensions, I console myself with the thought that I saw more bad films in Yorkshire in eighteen months than I should wish to see again in a lifetime.

But I often regret the absence of the little man in the blue dungarees into whose hand I pressed so many sixpences, and I shall never forget the look of despair on his face when I arrived for a bath once just before Christmas. 'Oh sir, you shouldn't have come tonight,' he said sorrowfully. 'I see people tonight I shan't see till this time next year.' Yes, there are hidden depths to that time-honoured cliché: 'Are you having your annual?'

Oxford Mail 11 February 1961

I am pleased to say the Victorian public baths in Albert Street, Keighley, are now a Grade II listed monument. They were first mooted in 1866 but did not open until ten years later after remaining half-built for six years because of escalating costs. I never ventured beyond the four first class slipper baths on the ground floor. Beyond them were first and second class swimming baths and a ladies' plunge bath. Upstairs were Turkish, first and second class slipper, plunge, shower and vapour baths.

Another feature was the washhouse, which by 1954 had twelve washing machines, twelve handwashing stalls, three hydro extractors, a steam-heated mangle and thirty-six clothes horses, plus a spin-drier housewives nicknamed The Buzz because of the noise it made.

The now obsolete phrase 'having your annual' – still commonplace in the 1960s – apparently dates from medieval times when people did literally bath once a year!

My first digs were in Sunny Mount off Highfield Lane 200 yards up the hill from the baths. The landlord was a

Dickensian character whose idea of joke was to sit on the loo in the dark with a rubber mask on his face at closing time. When new lodgers came home from the pub bursting for a pee, as they often did, and made a bee-line for the W.C. he would frighten the life out of them.

Revisiting the 'flu

After snuffling my way through Christmas, it may seem ridiculous to wax sentimental about a flu bug but, I must confess, I began to feel better the minute they told me the little fellow I was suffering the side effects of was a close relative of the virus that rampaged around Britain ten years ago.

You see, it was on the Asian Flu Epidemic of 1957 that I could be said to have cut my journalistic teeth or perhaps rather more appropriately to have polished my newshound's nose. At the time, as a trainee journalist in the West Riding of Yorkshire, it was my daily chore to file a report on the latest situation to our Bradford evening paper, the *Telegraph and Argus*, and once a week write a more detailed survey for my own paper, the *Keighley News*.

One by one my colleagues succumbed to the disease, but by some miracle I escaped and as the weeks went by it became a standing joke in the office that I was being spared by the bugs in order that I might keep up the flow of propaganda for their campaign. Perhaps I was. Who knows?

On the eve of my departure on a two-week holiday to Spain with my friend, Chris Prior, I handed over the story to another junior member of the staff and immediately sensed the first symptoms I had learned to describe so well. But retiring to bed with a hot drink and a couple of aspirins and staying there for the next few days was out of the question.

At ten o'clock that night I climbed out of the hottest bath I have ever had, donned four sweaters, two pairs of trousers, a thick woollen scarf and a cap, stuffed the gas meter full of shillings, swallowed four Beecham's powders and a tumbler full of rum, prayed for deliverance and pulled the bedclothes over my head.

In the morning I felt fine and for the next twenty-four hours I basked in a wonderful glow of euphoria. It was not until we reached Rouen and were standing by the roadside vainly trying to thumb a lift that I realised I had not shaken the fever off. Quite how ill I was I cannot now remember, but I do know on Bordeaux Station while I was bending my fevered head over a cold tap in order to ease my sore throat, a peasant came up to me, made me take a swig from his wine bottle, and thrust a loaf in my hand.

As the third class carriage we had managed to scrape up the fare for trundled into Irun the fever began to lift and, under the influence of a warm Spanish sun, in a day or two had completely disappeared. For the next fortnight we lived in luxury on 10s 6d a day, washing down fine meals with long draughts of cool wine.

It was thus with a distinct feeling of guilt on the homeward journey I observed near the frontier the noble Spaniards sniffing and wiping their noses on the backs of their hands. Was I the wicked carrier who had brought La

Grippe they kept muttering bewilderedly about to the land where the pocket-handkerchief was unnecessary? Was I the thoughtless traveller who had introduced the scourge of Northern Europe to the cold-less South?

Back in Keighley I resumed my daily bulletins and weekly roundups until one afternoon, noticing me with my head in my hands and no doubt imagining I had had too long a session in the Lord Rodney the night before, the kindly news editor, Charlie Senior, said: 'Take the newsletter for Bradford to the station, lad, then you can go home.'

For the next fortnight I did not leave my bed and refused every potion my longsuffering landlady proffered me until she hit upon the notion of feeding me blackcurrant juice liberally laced with rum.

Asian flu, Mini-flu, Maxi-flu, whatever they call it, is an unpleasant, cunning illness, which holds you fast in its grip, tricks you into thinking you are getting better, then lays you low again with another dose of its deadly germs. But, if you will pardon me while I sneeze and add another spoonful of sugar to my steaming mug of non-alcoholic lemon juice, you will understand why a nostalgic, slightly delirious smile spreads across my face when anyone mentions it.

Oxford Mail 6 January 1968

4 – Trainee journalist: Swindon

*After the cheerful bonhomie of Keighley, the failure of the
Swindon Evening Advertiser to keep pace with the times
was a shock. Towards the end of the eleven months that I
was there, the editor, David More, got a rocket from head
office. The population of the town had shot up by 10,000
as it expanded to accommodate the London overspill. The
paper had not added a single copy to its circulation.*

*I was dispatched to remedy the situation. The newspa-
per had no contacts on any of the new estates. I went from
door to door, piecing together what was meant to be an
in-depth survey.*

*The minute my first article appeared the team behind
the development, who had refused to co-operate, changed
their tune. Thanks to the frankness with which they
talked about the trials and errors of what proved to be a
remarkably successful social experiment I was able to
produce a series of features that hopefully helped the
incomers to feel wanted. I was no longer around to know.
The Westminster Press had transferred me to Oxford.*

The Midas touch

My mother-in-law asked me to see if I could find her a couple of sprigs of mimosa in the village the other day. Luckily, the Forge Flower Shop had just two left. Marvelling how a bloom from warmer climes that must have travelled a considerable distance to icy Eynsham could be so cheap, I handed over my £1.80 and returned triumphantly with my purchase. A tradition dating back sixty years had been upheld. Every anniversary since her marriage apart from the war years, my mother-in-law has endeavoured to have a bunch of mimosa in the house to remind her of the flowers she carried in her bouquet on her wedding day.

Originally the delicate green fronds speckled with scores of tiny yellow pompoms came from the south of France, but in these days of Interflora, global air travel and hothouse cultivation, I suppose they might come from anywhere. I myself have seen cascades at the roadside in Western Australia, as if King Midas had touched the trees in passing, and only weeks ago I spotted a clump growing wild on the hillside in Southern Spain.

In fact, in recent years it was not the availability of the bloom that exercised my mother-in-law and my dear departed father-in-law. It was whether their order would make the eighty-five-mile journey from Inverness to the west coast.

Living in the Highlands of Scotland, there was always the risk in January that a sudden fall of snow might cut them off from the rest of civilisation. As a fail-safe my wife, Sue, would buy a few sprigs of mimosa locally, wrap them carefully, and dispatch them by first class mail a few days before the anniversary, in the hopes that if the florist failed to make it, the postie might still get through. In the event, both consignments always reached their destination, however atrocious the weather, serving in a small but appealing way to underline the continuation of a long and happy marriage.

Oddly enough, until I became involved in helping to ensure there was an adequate supply to mark this important family occasion, my only experience of mimosa was a surfeit of the stuff when I was a junior reporter on the *Evening Advertiser*.

In 1958 the Swindon and District branch of the National Union of Journalists asked me to do the decor for their annual Press Ball in Marlborough Town Hall. The ballroom itself needed little titivation; indeed, my only contribution was to dissuade the Woman's Editor from knocking picture hooks into its elegant oak-panelled walls.

The chamber beneath it, where the drinks and buffet were to be served, was a different matter, with its six large, ugly, curtainless windows. My solution was to fill these with cartoon panels depicting the unlikely uses to which readers put our newspapers, ranging from a tramp sleeping under one on a park bench to the proverbial string of torn-up sheets on a nail behind the privy door.

I could make the panels out of wooden battens and end-reels of newsprint on the day of the ball, but who would draw the cartoons? A seventeen-year-old who had joined the paper straight from school two weeks earlier, assured me he would have no difficulty translating my crude notebook sketches into elegant outsize drawings.

Meanwhile, the chairman of the Press Ball committee kept burbling on about a consignment of mimosa he had been promised by a Swindon florist. At that stage I'm not sure I knew what mimosa was.

The seventeen-year-old was as good as his word. As fast as I knocked up the panels, he decorated them with bold, eye-catching caricatures. About an hour before the ball was due to begin, we stood back to admire our handiwork. There was an anxious tap on my shoulder. The chairman of the Press Ball committee said: 'Don, it's arrived.'

'What's arrived?' 'The mimosa!' There were boxes of it. Too much to fill vases. Too late to turn into bouquets for all the ladies. I raised my eyes to the heavens in despair, and as I lowered them again received the answer to my prayers: the polished oak staircase leading to the ballroom.

We swathed each side of the stair-carpet in mimosa, and as I left to pick up my dress suit from my digs in Swindon, the first guests were treading delightedly up the steps in a cloud of golden pompoms. My motor scooter developed a puncture. I had to hire a taxi, and by the time I returned the ball was almost over. But the congratulations... 'Don, those cartoons. Brilliant! And that mimosa. Out of this world!'

Witney Gazette 1 February 1996

It's a dog's life

Believe it or not, both these incidents happened in Swindon within days of one another exactly as I describe them, the first in Victoria Road, the second in Dixon Street, where I was lodging.

Late one night as I left the office and padded across the deserted street, I noticed a couple in the doorway of a chemist's shop. There is nothing unusual about couples canoodling in darkened doorways. But as I drew nearer, I was forced onto tiptoe. The young lady was kneeling in supplication to a weighing machine and the young man – with much cursing and striking of matches – was feeding pennies into it.

Silently I took up a post of observation behind the convenient awning of a nearby butcher's shop and watched this pretty spectacle. The object of it, as I soon discovered, was to weigh a dog.

Poor beast! It was by the obvious characteristics of its doleful eyes, its floppy ears, its domed forehead, its sloppy face, its hangdog look, a spaniel and by far the largest creature of that species I have ever seen.

With difficulty it perched with four paws on a tiny platform intended for two feet. With enviable patience it attempted to lick its mistress's face and, whenever it succeeded, its ruddered rump slid wagging to the ground or its two forepaws splayed sideways, driving its damp nose into the weighing machine stanchion.

The rebukes it received for these incontrollable outbursts

of affection were paralleled by the relations of its human attendants. Tempers had clearly reached fraying point long before I arrived.

Each time the spaniel had been persuaded to balance itself like a performing elephant at the circus, the girl would cry: 'Now!' Her boyfriend would drop a penny into the slot and strike a match. The needle would spin round the briefly illumined dial and before it hovered to a halt the match-end would be dropped with a cry of pain or the dog would be forced to lick and slip.

How many pennies were spent in vain that night I do not know. But at length the young man announced with an oath: 'We've run out,' and the girl, sighing sadly, stood up and scanned the street for possible new supplies.

I slipped away into the night. That dog had suffered enough. Why should they be so surreptitious about the operation, I asked myself as I resumed my homeward path? Why should they not weigh it in broad daylight? Why should they weigh it at all?

I admit that it was overweight. I admit that it had a waddle more in keeping with a pampered dachshund. But who cared? The thought of its grossness being eventually established in hard stones and pounds and – who knows the diabolical intentions of intransigent dog-owners? – diminished by a diet, kept me awake most of the night.

Reflecting on the incident in the cold light of day, I realised how much pets are at the mercy of human beings. As a puppy, that spaniel must have been nurtured on indigestible titbits, deprived of exercise, until its elephantine proportions became more than a joke: an embarrassment even to its foolish owners.

But seemingly there is no end to the indignities to which man's best friend may be submitted. A few nights later I returned to my lodgings to find myself locked out. As always, the front door was ajar. But the hall door immediately beyond it had been slammed too hard by one of my fellow-lodgers and its simple catch had fallen to.

Not anxious to disturb my landlady, I tried the back door, then the front window of my ground floor bedroom. Neither would budge. I shook the hall door. It remained fast. In despair I rang the bell. There was no answer from the silent house.

I skirted the flowerbeds of the front garden and pressed my fingers into the crevices of my bedroom window frame. While I was involved in this suspicious-looking operation, the familiar tread of legal feet echoed along the street. Guiltily, I scuttled back into the porch. They drew nearer and stopped. Had I been discovered? No, they were off again.

I breathed a sigh of relief. Wait a minute though! They were coming back. Heavens, I thought, I *have* been discovered. For the next five minutes I lived in constant dread, as they paced back and forth, stopping at regular intervals that could mean only one thing: I must give myself up.

At last, I crept out, still rehearsing a carefully worded explanation, to behold by the pale light of the moon, not a policeman, but a drunken old man staggering along the opposite pavement in hobnailed boots, trailing an unwilling mongrel on an enormous length of string. The street lamps were out and he had forgotten where he lived.

Now and then he paused and felt the numbers on the gateposts. Now and then he ventured up a garden path. But doubt always got the better of decision and he staggered back into the street to resume his bewildered wanderings. The dog showed not the slightest interest in any of these adventures, but persistently dragged his master to the gate of no. thirty-five. As persistently, his master dragged him away again.

Finally, he dragged the reluctant beast to the door of no. thirty-seven, peered through the letterbox, and having reassured himself, rang the bell. There was no reply. He rang again, then a third time and a fourth, still no reply. Wearily, he faced about and sat on the step.

The liquid at war with his senses erupted in a fearful belch and as if by magic a light appeared above the doorway of no. thirty-five. His search was over. A young woman burst into the street, snatched the mongrel from his fumbling hands, and bundled him brusquely up his own pathway. The door slammed. I heaved at my bedroom window and it flew open with an answering shriek.

Next day I saw the mongrel taking himself for a walk and remarked on the truth of the saying: 'It's a dog's life.' He pretended not to hear me.

Oxford Mail 1 April 1961

While I was at Swindon I went on another continental holiday with Chris Prior, this time first to Belgium to visit the Brussels World Fair, then to Germany to take a cruise on a Rhine paddle steamer from Cologne to

Bare entertainment

When I tell people the only strip shows I have seen have been by accident, they look at me with an old-fashioned smile and say: 'Oh, yes!' But it happens to be true. At the first St. Giles's Fair after the Second World War my parents took me to a sideshow and from that rather tawdry experience my lack of interest in that particular form of theatrical entertainment dates.

Although I was only twelve at the time, I sensed the embarrassment they felt at unwittingly exposing their son to a display of female nudity and I remember a whispered conversation in which they debated whether they should stay or try to push their way out of the packed marquee. Actually, they needn't have bothered. The idea of watching a lady in her birthday suit performing static victory poses behind a gilt frame, screened by a white sheet you could only just see through, didn't appeal very much to me. I preferred the chap who juggled with knives.

All of thirteen years later during an idyllic holiday cruising down the Rhine it rained one evening and my friend, Chris Prior, and I sought refuge in a cinema in Cologne. We had no idea what to see because we couldn't read the posters and the glass panels containing the film stills were all steamed up, so we chose the establishment with the longest queue outside, paid our money, and presently the programme began with a hoary documentary.

We thought we must be attending a thinly disguised meeting of neo-Nazi Party members until after fifteen long, boring minutes the film ended and the lights went up. On to the stage stepped a beautiful girl in furs and long black gloves, a piano struck up in the pit, and she went into a seductive, adroitly executed routine during which at intervals she divested herself of her apparel. Then the lights went down again and another hoary documentary started flickering across the screen.

In my time as a drama critic I have known moments when you really could drop a pin in a theatre and hear it fall and others when the audience have literally been on the edge of their seats, but I have never known an atmosphere as electric as existed in that cinema that night before her fifth and final appearance.

Being Englishmen, we thought it all rather funny and the next night went to one of those dance halls, then a novelty, when you sat at a table with a telephone and if you saw a girl who took your fancy, you dialled her number and asked her to dance. Nobody seemed to be dialling anybody. They just sat around looking miserable like they do at provincial English dance halls when they're playing an old-fashioned foxtrot.

We walked across to the bar and after a couple of beers discovered that there was a secret mirrored door at the end of it, through which the cognoscenti seemed to be disappearing into another, more exotic room. It was no different to the first room actually except there were cloths on the tables and candles, and the drinks cost twice as much.

Of the succession of girls who performed in the next

half-hour I remember very little apart from the fact that they all looked tired and skinny and I would probably remember nothing at all if it hadn't been for Texa.

Texa was different. She was plump like a rubber ball, she frolicked with the chubby innocence nudes in a sylvan setting do in Old Masters' paintings and, just for a moment, she made me believe there might be an art to striptease after all.

At the conclusion of her act, she flung aloft the two pink balloons she had held tightly clasped to her bosom throughout her somewhat unrewarding excursion into the realms of Terpsichore and, for a fleeting seconds, they hovered in the air above her outstretched arms while in perfect counterpoint two podgy pink buttocks hovered below.

Yet the odd thing is when I try to explain the aesthetic appeal of that moment, the sheer poetry of it, to genuine connoisseurs of striptease, they look at me with an old-fashioned smile and say: 'Oh yes!' and I feel like a little boy again at St. Giles' Fair.

Weekend Oxford Mail 13 January 1968

5 – The move to Oxford

Knowing I was a local boy and a graduate to boot it made sense to transfer me to the Oxford Mail and Times when they needed a reporter at short notice. It created panic at the Evening Advertiser. I still had the last article in my series on Swindon New Town to write. You'll have to take your notebook with you, the news editor said, and post the piece to us.

Fond as I had become of the charcoal sketch of Richard Jefferies above my desk, the famous Wiltshire naturalist who had started life as a junior reporter on the Advertiser in the nineteenth century and, legend had it, sometimes forgot the story he was supposed to be writing if he came across a pond on his way to an assignment, it was a relief to swap the bumbling inefficiency of Swindon for the professionalism of Oxford.

As news reporter, university correspondent, columnist, feature writer, theatre critic and arts editor in turn and often a combination of all five, I enjoyed a charmed life in what was a golden age for provincial journalism.

I was to cover a succession of memorable stories from Sir Winston Churchill's burial to the Great Train

Robbery, but it was my relish for the ridiculous and the offbeat that first caught the eye of my fellow journalists.

Easter egg race

With a close finish the annual presidential Easter egg race held by the Junior Common Room of St. Peter's Hall – *destined to become St. Peter's College* – in the main quadrangle ended in victory for the retiring president, Mr Harold Burnett. The president-elect, Mr Albert Johnson, was disqualified for failing to eat his egg at the finishing line.

The race, for which conditions are laid down in an ancient document, allegedly dug up by a college gardener, was held in perfect conditions and was watched by a large crowd of undergraduates and their girlfriends.

In the traditional fashion the event was started by a trumpet blown from an upper window by the Herald Extraordinary, Mr Timothy Lusty. The two competitors were assembled by the Sentinel of the Stoup, Mr Peter Holmes, and were led to the starting line dressed in top hats and blue and white striped pyjamas by their seconds, Mr John Widdowson and Mr Tony Augarde. The Warden of the Glove, Mr David George, then descended by a rope from the roof of the college and presented Mr Burnett with the gauntlet, which he proceeded to throw at the feet of Mr Johnson.

Mr Johnson received the challenge and the race was on. The Warden of the Egg, Mr Alan Smith, appeared leading two white ducks across the lawn by strings. They were tethered and he returned to the starting line to present the competitors with eggs and spoons.

Mr Burnett went straight into the lead on the first stage down which they had to roll their eggs. But he somewhat overshot the corner and Mr Johnson gained ground on the south side of the quad, which they ran with their eggs in their spoons.

The ducks had to be steered along the east side of the quad. The final stage was cycled by the competitors, neck and neck. They also finished fifty hula hoop revolutions together.

Mr Burnett, declared the winner, was presented with a stoup of ale. By way of consolation, he presented Mr Johnson with a chocolate Easter egg. Mr Johnson replied: 'Sir, your kindness exceeds your beauty,' and the ceremonies were at an end for another year.

Oxford Mail 13 March 1959

The race, within days of me joining the Oxford Mail, took place across New Inn Hall Street from Newspaper House. My story made the front page, a rare event for an offbeat local story in those days.

Wrestling returns to Oxford Town Hall

Tibor Szakacs rolled through the red, white and blue ropes and landed with a sickening thump on the Press table. A sweaty back printed itself across my notebook, smudging my inane scribblings and flattening my packet of cigarettes. A voice in the crowd cried: 'Go easy. That's the Press!'

Szakacs straightened himself with a grunt of contempt and rolled back into the ring. A smart pat on the black rump and the struggle continued. The square strip of canvas, gleaming like a desert under the white arc lamps, once more began to edge towards me as it rebounded with the thwack of falling bodies and sprawling limbs. Wrestling had returned to Oxford Town Hall.

'They call that sport, humph!' snorted a colleague from his safer position at the end of the table. The tight-packed crowd obviously did. There were loud boos when the promoter, Mr Johnny Dale, called for a round of applause for the members of the City Council sitting opposite. After all, they had given only tentative approval to this form of entertainment and as one wag pointed out: 'They've got free seats.'

He ought to have been in the bar at the interval, which due to the superior skill of Harry Kendall, the deaf-mute from London, fell punctually at nine, when Councillor Mrs Florence Wood confessed: yes, perhaps she had been wrong to vote against it. 'I am surprised,' she said, taking a bite out of a spam sandwich, 'this professional wrestling is quite good. In fact, I think it's clever the way they throw themselves about. Of course, I was more worried about the crowd, but they seem very well-behaved.'

The Deputy Chief Constable, Superintendent Leonard North, added his approval. They were a 'very orderly bunch,' he said.

Wrestling, according to the *Encyclopaedia Britannica*, 'is one of the most primitive and universal of sports'. The Egyptians did it. The Greeks did it. The Romans did it. And now, in a more civilised way, everybody does it. But don't ask me to explain. I, like forty per cent of the spectators, in the estimate of the referee, Lou Marco, was a novice to the game. But I should learn.

This dapper little man in the black shirt and evening trousers, who once beat the panel of the television quiz show *What's My Line?* and starred as the referee in the wrestling bout in the film *A Kid for Two Farthings*, opined: 'I think wrestling has come to stay in Oxford.'

In which event I will put before you what little knowledge I gleaned from my first encounter last night. There are two contestants, who having entered the ring at opposite corners, wiped their feet on a doormat nearly as shaggy as their chests and had their boots and nails inspected by the referee, perform a muscular pas-de-deux with a little rock 'n' roll thrown in.

There are four or six ten-minute rounds and the object seems to be for one of them to tie the other in such a knot of pain that he is forced to submit, press his shoulders to the canvas long enough for the referee, who is also allowed inside, to cry: 'Wurrah, two-ah' and hammer on the floor, or to knock an opponent out with a blow delivered with the back of the hand somewhere between the chin and the chest.

The subtleties include manifold holds and throws. 'That was the flying mare,' John Parsons, the expert, told me at one point. But if it had been the scissors, the wrestler's bridge, or reverse head chancery, as the programme kindly listed them, it would have been all the same to me.

All I know is that eight men took part in the evening's entertainment, and that apart from odd moments when bodies tangled in rubber ropes leapt towards me and made me bite the end off my cigarette, when flying boots came close enough to make me smell the resin on them, or when spit and sweat spattered about my innocent ears, I enjoyed it.

Oxford Mail 17 November 1960

Punt jousting

The rules, said the announcer, 'may be amended, subtracted from or added to at any moment' – and they were, before five soggy he-men from St. Edmund Hall emerged as champions of the punt-jousting tournament at Marston Ferry.

Twice the punts had sunk, the icy Cherwell had claimed an untold number of jousters, both poles had snapped in the fray, and one gentleman rested supine under a willow tree. It is perhaps not pertinent to inquire into the reason for his collapse.

The trophy – a two-foot high black and orange toucan, presented by the sponsors* – last seen in the hands of the Brasenose College team, one of whose number yelled: 'We declare Teddy Hall the winners,' (their way of protesting at the inability of Keble College to admit defeat) had long since vanished in a grey Mini Minor up the bumpy track that leads to Marston Ferry Road.

Thus, the victors were left with the cold consolation of replenishing their glasses with the dark brown fluid manufactured by the sponsors, toasting themselves, wringing out their sodden garments and retiring to the comfort of the bathtub.

The event had started quietly enough with the three judges, the American rugby Blue, Peter Dawkins, the English President of the University Boat Club, Mike Davies, and a dour Scotsman from Balliol, Brian Baird, ensconced under parasols on the bank below the *Victoria Arms*.

Brasenose met Lincoln in the first heat and after some hesitation about positions, the punts were turned back to

---

* Guinness adopted the toucan in 1935 when they asked the advertising agency S.H. Benson to provide them with an upmarket campaign. The artist was John Gilroy and among the agency's copywriters was the crime novelist Dorothy L. Sayers. They dropped the toucan when they left the agency in 1982 but it remains much loved and is still available in special editions and on T-shirts.

Punt jousting is alleged to have begun in Cambridge, where it still takes place. It was originally an inter-varsity sport, but now the Cambridge team accepts challenges from all-comers. Traditionally Cambridge punters operate from the platform end of their craft, Oxford punters from the other end.

front, the four paddlers of each team crouched two abreast, and the two jousters with their ten-foot poles [*a pad used to score hits and prevent injuries with the end of them*], balanced precariously on the platform at the rear.

At the end of each tilt the jouster either clambered down the boat or retrieved himself from the river while his place was taken by a colleague. And so, after six tilts – the fifth was indecisive – Brasenose emerged as heat-winners, Lincoln having taken two duckings to their one.

Then came Keble versus New College and the trouble began. At the fourth tilt the punts met with a sickening thud, the Keble jouster was knocked in and retaliated by pulling the New College man after him. Dazed by these rough tactics New College succumbed 2–1 at the sixth tilt. Finally in the first round Worcester met St. John's and again the score was 2–1, this time in Worcester's favour.

Into the semi-finals a new team was introduced: St. Edmund Hall, whose punt after three tilts at Brasenose sank under their weight and the water it had shipped by another team in the previous round. Not to be outdone Brasenose too disappeared beneath the waves and much baling with a biscuit tin ensued before the tournament could continue and Teddy Hall squeezed their way into the final 3–2.

Alas, the second semi-final was a fiasco and ended in a free-for-all between Worcester and Keble when the score was still 0–0 after eleven tilts, whereupon both teams were disqualified and a new team introduced – the Charon Club – to joust against St. Edmund Hall in the final.

These, the invincible men of Teddy Hall vanquished

2–0, then climbed ashore, only to be requested to re-embark to meet the disgruntled men of Keble in a three-tilt challenge heat. 'We know you'll beat them,' said the organiser reassuringly. They did, 2–0.

Later in the term, it is said, after a similar preliminary on the Cam, they will represent Oxford University against Cambridge. But for the moment they are only interested in finding their toucan.

Oxford Mail 15 May 1962

Polo at Kirtlington

On a warm Sunday you may find more than a 1,000 people at Kirtlington Park to watch the polo. Yesterday afternoon it was cold and perhaps 200 motorists paid their ten-bobs to line the ground.

The most ancient of games with stick and ball – the earliest record of it is in Persia in 525BC – was introduced to England in 1869 by the Tenth Hussars and a year or two later an account of the first public game of 'hockey on horseback,' played on Hounslow Heath, appeared in the pages of the *Morning Post*.

The Kirtlington Park and Oxford University Polo Club was founded in 1928, folded during the Second World War, but was revived in 1952. It had seventy non-playing members, who subscribed £2 each year to watch the twenty-two playing members in action, but there were many more casual spectators.

It owed its success partly to the prowess of the Duke of Edinburgh on a polo pony and the consequent attention the game had received from television, partly to the keenness of the Budgett family, who owned Kirtlington Park, and club secretary Brigadier G.H. Fanshawe, a 'well-known high-goal player' before the Second World War.

'High-goal' we learnt from the commentator, Mr G.H. Sheppard, temporarily forced out of the game by a poisoned hand, meant good enough to have a heavy handicap.

All players are handicapped and sometimes a particularly good side starts with a deficit of three or four goals. But yesterday, as the handicap of both Kirtlington Park and their opponents, the Household Brigade Polo Club, is six, they started equal.

The ground is 300 yards long and 160 yards wide with a crimson board running down each side and two beflagged goal posts ten feet high and eight yards apart at each end. The four players in each team line up opposing one another at the centre and the umpire tosses the white wooden ball into the ruck.

The match is under way. The air re-echoes with the chock of ball against polo-stick. The turf reverberates with the drum of thundering hooves. The cool voice of the commentator is interrupted by cries of 'Follow the ball in' 'Come on, gentlemen, pitch into them.'

Between 'chukkers' – there are four 'chukkers' or seven-and-half minute periods to each game – Mr Sheppard told us that it is not a poor man's sport. 'You can't buy a made polo pony under £300 and some cost more. Then there's the keep, say £3 to £4 a week, not to mention your gear,' and one pony is not enough. You need two ponies for one match, playing alternate 'chukkers'.

Most players have at least three and all the big players have five or six. Captain S.J. Loder of the Household Brigade had seven we learnt from his stud groom, fifty-three-year-old Laurie Scott, from Buckhurst Park, near Ascot. As he unbuckled the shin-pads of Captain Loder's grey mount, The Rabbit – 'worth £1,000 at least, a very fast pony' – he gave us the story of polo from the horse's mouth, based on a lifetime's experience with polo ponies.

'They love it,' he said, slapping The Rabbit's rump and telling her to move over. 'They enjoy it as much as a footballer does football. As soon as they see the ball, they're after it. Of course, you do get the bad ones, but these, I wouldn't dare leave one at home in the stables.'

The Kirtlington Park team was having a good afternoon and they were leading 7–1 when the match ended. What was the attraction of polo we asked one of the younger spectators as she queued for a cup of tea. 'Oh, I don't know,' she said. 'The excitement, the speed, the horsemanship, the horses, I've been fond of horses for as long as I can remember.'

Oxford Mail 21 May 1962

6 – Personal Columns

My first editor was Harford Thomas, who had been the Press Association's political correspondent. He was a hard news man who turned a typical provincial evening paper into a respected journal Fleet Street sat up and took notice of.

The industry, like the Oxford area and the rest of Britain, was still finding its feet after the Second World War, which meant advertising was scarce and paging tight. Despite Tory premier Harold Macmillan's boast that the majority of Britons had never had it so good it was to be the 1960s before the Oxford Mail really began to expand.

Even so, HT, as he was known, was keen on a Monday Music Page, a Tuesday Entertainments Page, and other slightly down-market features to provide a leaven of culture to the serious editorials and political commentaries he favoured for the leader page. Saturday was different. In addition to the profiles of leading local figures he encouraged reporters to contribute their personal views on events that were happening locally and nationally.

The big bang

On Friday 10 February 1961 Martin Ryle, Fellow of the Royal Society and Professor of Radio Astronomy at Cambridge, produced some startling evidence to the Royal Astronomical Society that the universe started with a bang. It has taken my simple layman's mind a fortnight to realise that that was how I thought it all began anyway.

Apparently, I have been missing out for the last thirteen years on a little joke shared between Thomas Gold and Herman Bondi at the other place in 1948, which subsequently became the deadly earnest theory that the universe was static.

Thank goodness I never knew. To have given to me in my formative years the idea that the universe would last for ever and then in 1961 to have it taken away again and replaced by the nasty notion that the whole thing was falling to bits might have come as a distinct blow.

As it is, I am quite unperturbed. I always thought all those galaxies were belting off into the blue like the shrapnel from a hand-grenade, that it was only a matter of time before the world slid like a rotten egg down the outer wall of space. Now I suppose I always shall unless some facetious don beside the Cam says to his neighbour: 'Heard that one about the Milky Way?' and his neighbour takes him seriously. Cambridge men never could appreciate a joke.

All the same, this fellow Ryle has got something with his radio telescope. Since radar came in, I have often wondered why they have persisted with those tubular monstrosities at the end of the pier, through which you pay a penny to look at the drizzle and the fog. How much more exciting it would be to peer at a green eye round which an illuminated windscreen-wiper swished mechanically, and have some informative know-all exclaim: 'See that speck there, that's the lighthouse. See that splodge there, that's your Aunt Annie taking a dip.'

Yes, you can throw away your brass telescopes. Radio's the thing for looking at things nowadays.

I first had an inkling of its possibilities as long ago as 1943 at the age of nine when I used to tinker with the knobs of our ancient wireless set and scare the life out of my ten-year-old neighbour by insisting that the peculiar noises which crackled through its aged loudspeaker were lost radio waves which had been drifting about in the atmosphere for years and had finally come to earth down our aerial.

I see now I was wrong. They were messages from different planets millions of light years away. But there I was, an innocent at large, stumbling on a scientific wonder which, had someone taken me seriously instead of threatening to stop my subscription to the *Wizard* and *Hotspur* comics if I didn't hold my tongue, might have put a stop to all this 'static' nonsense before it ever started.

Well, my chance of glory passed me by. What other scientific interest I had dwindled to a shabby credit in School Certificate and I took to Latin and Greek to escape the smell of burning sulphur and my habit of breaking test-tubes. Now I am just an ignorant observer not fit enough even to be shot into space as a human guinea pig.

Still, I don't begrudge Professor Ryle his success, and I envy him his telescope, which they say is several times more sensitive than the bowl-shaped telescope at Joddrell Bank.

It is not only the thought of being able to twiddle a knob and pick up a pair of galaxies in collision 500m. light years away that excites me. It is the dream of travelling back through time eight million years. Just imagine what it would be like if your newspaper boy had to cycle round the world to deliver your copy of the *Oxford Mail*: how fascinating it would be to read news two or three years – sorry, eighty days – old. Or remember the many, many times you have pulled up the linoleum and sat until the small hours engrossed in yellowing newsprint.

Because of a silly scientific phenomenon known as the speed of travel and the time it takes the waves these radio-active stars emit to reach Professor Ryle's telescope, they are ages old when they arrive. They are history presented live in the here and now.

In fact, this squabble between Independent Television and the British Broadcasting Corporation about the third channel is ludicrous. What we want is that telescope harnessed to our screens with a running commentary from an astronomical Richard Dimbleby. It would mean staying up at unearthly hours on occasions if we wanted to catch some grand event in the pageant of our evolution. It might clash now and then with *Wells Fargo* or *Sunday Night at the Palladium*.

But wouldn't it be worth it? It is all very well for an earthbound poet like T.S. Eliot to write: 'This is the way the world ends, not with a bang but a whimper.' But by Zeus – if you will excuse a Greek expression – imagine what it would be like if, one night, all our cathode-ray tubes were lit by the bang with which creation started.

Oxford Mail 24 February 1961

Treading on eggshells

Since Christmas, when I abandoned the last of the medicated shampoos, I have been washing my hair with what I now suspect to be a concentration of reject marmalade lemons, dirty detergent and runny egg. And the sad thing is I would never have known but for the rumpus there has been about the Egg Marketing Board's* stockpile of 4,000 tons of frozen liquid egg.

Upon learning that the only bags of the stuff they had managed to sell were to a mink farm and a shampoo firm, I hastily examined my locks, which are deciduous, for any signs of exceptional fall-out. But ladies who have just bought fur coats can rest assured. If it hasn't wrought havoc with my tender capillaries, then there is not the slightest

* The Government set up the Egg Marketing Board in 1956 to stabilise the market for eggs after a nationwide collapse in sales. The Board purchased all eggs produced in the UK, graded them and marketed them, stamping each egg with a lion logo as a guarantee of quality. The board closed in 1971 to be superseded by the British Egg Industry Council in 1986. Its Egg Information Service revived the lion logo in 1998.

chance of their status symbols moulting for the next twenty years at least. All the same, the discovery has come as a distinct shock.

For the last six months I have been anointing my head with what I fondly imagined was the *crème supreme* of tonsorial unguents. Each time I took down the bottle of egg and lemon shampoo from the shelf a picture would come into my mind of a shampoo dairy somewhere in Somerset where well-scrubbed maids in chiffon shifts squeezed the last oozings of sun-drenched lemons, won at great cost on the battle-scarred slopes of Cyprus, cracked and poured with Mrs Beeton-like prodigality the golden yolks of dozens of new-laid eggs and, letting rich soapflakes fall the while like snow into their basins, refined the substance with their own lilywhite hands into a subtle cream.

But spare your tears, stout hearts, it is not so. The whole lot is probably turned out by some bald old josser in Wapping. 'Fill the copper, mother,' he says to his wife before he goes off to his nightshift at Billingsgate. 'Ask the dustmen to send over the sack of old rind they promised me, and go round to the butchers and get that bag of liquid egg out of the freezer.'

Then back he comes in the dismal dawn, runs the vile mess through his fishy fingers, strains off the lumps, turns on the tap, and fills drum after seven-pound drum, which some smoother middle-man later palms off on the trade with a smart tongue and an expense account luncheon. Life is full of deceptions.

But not even that hardboiled symbol of wholesomeness, the little lion, I notice, will lend his name to the Egg

Board's latest product. He still appears on their eggs, and he would appear on their best quality edible egg as well, if it had a shell. Lion brand they call it. But with this stuff they cannot get rid of he will have nothing to do, so they have been forced to dream up another name: 'industrial melange'.

Why industrial I don't know, unless there was a crisis brewing in the Middle East when it first started piling up and they thought they might sell it off as heavy grade oil. I can just see factory lathes turning out nuts and bolts at one end and omelettes at the other.

But as a student of sauce bottle French myself, I know where the melange comes from. 'Cette sauce de haute qualité est un melange...'* and at that point I can hear some publicity-minded minion from Runny Egg Health To The Danger Of screaming with delight: 'Melange! Melange! That's it. Quick! What does it mean, dear? Turn the bottle round.'

And upon reading the English translation: 'blend', going into rapture, kissing his broody little spouse on both cheeks, and dashing back to headquarters to inform the top brass of his discovery, and not one of them bothering to consult a French-English lexicon, where they would have found the alternative rendering 'mess'.

Industrial mess! Well, never mind. That just about sums

* HP Sauce, which takes its name from the Houses of Parliament depicted on its label, for many years had a description in French of the brown sauce in its bottle on one side and a translation in English on the opposite side. It was the only French many children and quite a few adults knew by heart!

it up for you and me. But what about the millions and millions of hens, who go to such enormous trouble to lay all these eggs and, thanks to the butterfingered farmhands and mutton-fisted packers, see their hard labours end up as part of a vast un-settable blancmange?

I've no doubt they would complain if they had the chance. We used to have three or four geese at home and they kicked up merry hell when we cracked open the eggs they had been sitting on for months and tipped out the very high-octane industrial melange.

But the hens have other things to think about at the moment. A firm of chicken breeders has just had a poultry husbandry research officer from Mytholmroyd in Yorkshire spend two hours each morning for ten days studying how the poor birds eat, and he has come up with the dreadful information that some of them are bullies and chase the others away from their food.

Maybe, of course, it was simply that they were showing off. After all, it is not every day that you have a human-being perched on your favourite roost watching everything you do. But assuming like most other things he was only a nine days' wonder, his findings on the tenth should be fairly reliable and, for myself, I am prepared to believe that the bullies enjoy a good leisurely tuck-in for an average of two minutes fifty-four seconds eighty-five times in twenty hours while the bullied have to dip in 128 times for an average of two minutes three seconds over the same period to assuage their hunger.

If the bullies can be persuaded to take a less vehement attitude to eating, and the firm manages to turn the thirty-seven million chicks it hopes to hatch in the next year into pullets that much quicker, all well and good. But has the Egg Marketing Board, I wonder, realised the implications of all this?

For it also means that all these pullets will be straining and crowing over their first eggs that much earlier, the shells of their adolescent offerings will be that much thinner, and there will be a lot, lot more industrial melange, and what are they going to do with it all?

Say that I and other public-spirited individuals dutifully lave our bonces three times a day with egg and lemon shampoo long after we are bald as coots, and say that a free mink coat is given away with every bottle to keep the women customers happy, there will still be oodles of the stuff left over. And no! No! Don't anybody suggest it! Whose grandmother is going to suck frozen liquid egg?

Oxford Mail June 1961

East-West conversation

The autumn before I left Swindon, I went to Bristol to take the National Council for the Training of Journalists proficiency test. Probably because so much was expected of me, I found it more daunting than my final examinations at Oxford and much to my landlady's consternation was unable to eat my breakfast before I set off.

The day passed in a dyspeptic haze. I need not have worried. On 15 December 1958 the Group Training

Officer, Philip Duncum, sent me a congratulatory note. 'Part I: interview 65%; copy 80; handout 90%; Part II (law), 81%; Part III – English, 75%; newspaper practice, 90%; current affairs, 88%. Very nice too.'

The same day I received a letter from the NCTJ director informing me I had won a one guinea book token for scoring the highest mark of the 136 candidates in the newspaper practice section. He added it was the third time in the last three years someone from the Wiltshire Newspaper Company had won. Wherever we got our expertise in newspaper practice it was not at Swindon!

After I arrived back in Oxford, I learnt I had won the Westminster Press Junior Journalist of the Year award: a month's holiday and £200 to spend. I fancied taking an exploratory trip to Japan but that proved impossible.

In the end I spent a month travelling round Greece in September 1960 with my then girlfriend Margaret Speight. We flew out by Olympic Airways and returned by the Simplon-Orient express, sadly not the luxury train of the Agatha Christie crime novel, but an altogether grubbier and overloaded form of travel.

If only, they always say, when another United Nations Assembly ends in stalemate, if only the ordinary Joe Bloggs each side of the Iron Curtain could meet and thrash things out. If only. The other week my girlfriend and I made a fourteen-hour journey from Belgrade to Venice. We had unwisely decided to travel by rail from Athens to London after a holiday in Greece.

In prospect, it had looked romantic enough. The

Simplon-Orient Express covers the long run to Paris in three days and nights and, we had thought, by stopping off at Salonika (now Thessaloniki), Belgrade and Venice we could soften the rigours of the journey and supplement it with the simple pleasure of sightseeing in those famous cities.

In fact, I caught food poisoning at the start of the journey and we spent a week shuttling from train to train in between mad midnight searches for hotels and hurried snatches of sleep to catch yet more trains.

Tired and weary, we boarded the express at Belgrade after a night in a Kafkaesque tenement building, whither we had been sent by the State Tourist Board after they had informed us all the city's hotels (they number no more than a dozen) were full. The other occupants of our compartment were a party of Bulgarians on their way to the Rome Olympic Games and an enormous Italian opera singer, who had – with difficulty and a generous overlap – squeezed herself into a corner seat.

Conversation was at first desultory as we sped through miles of collective farms, admiring the impressive use of every inch of space, the herds of cattle, pigs, geese with their attendant family of peasants on every scrap of waste land, the unending procession of small boys making the same ribald salutation with the same unmentionable portion of their bodies. But as night fell these passing spectacles became too dark to see and attention turned inward.

On a dreadful journey from Salonika to Belgrade, when ten people squeezed into a compartment intended for eight and hundreds more squashed themselves into an impenetrable mass in the corridor, we had ended, after complicated exchanges in eleven different languages, by appending our signatures to the Latin tag – *Vita cara est cum collegis* – Life is precious when you have friends.

This night the real conversation began when the Bulgarians' young interpreter noticed us conversing between ourselves in English and joined in. He had studied some English at Sofia while becoming proficient in French for his present position and was anxious to try it out on us.

The routine questions: homes, our ages, our wages – extracted half in French, half in English – gave place in time to more general inquiries and soon we were joined by a stubby Bulgarian with dark, curly hair, whose French was even more primitive than ours, but whose attentions were obviously friendly.

'The *Daily Worker*,' he beamed in broken English upon learning I was a journalist. 'The *Daily Worker* is a good newspaper, no?' I said, yes, it was a nicely laid-out newspaper. 'But people read the *Daily Worker*?' 'Yes, some people.' 'Not everybody?' His Communist face expressed concern. Gently, I tried to explain the difficulties of the *Daily Worker's* circulation, where it stood in relation to other English newspapers, the gamut of a press that at the other extreme could include the *New Daily*. It did not register.

He shifted his attack. 'Harry Pollitt,' he smiled with new enthusiasm. 'What has happened to Harry Pollitt?' I said Harry Pollitt was dead. He rattled off the names of other English Communists. The known were registered with mutual smiles. The unknown filled him with dismay.

He retired, vaguely hurt. 'Anthony Eden,' our curly-headed friend said at length, recovering his joviality or perhaps having finally remembered the name he had been searching for. 'What has happened to Anthony Eden?' I said he had retired and was living in the country, that he was a sick man. The interpreter translated. 'Sick with the Suez?' came the triumphant rejoinder. I replied that Sir Anthony was already sick at the time of Suez, but that perhaps Suez had not helped.

The admission eased the atmosphere. 'And Winston Churchill,' he asked. 'What has happened to him?' I told him Sir Winston had also retired, but still held his seat in the House of Commons. 'My friend is a great admirer of Winston Churchill,' the interpreter diplomatically intervened. I replied that he was a great man, a great speech-maker and a great writer.

What books had Sir Winston Churchill written, he wanted to know? Could I send him copies? He would like to read them. I said that if he would like to give me his name and address, I would try, but it would depend on whether the Bulgarian authorities permitted the sending of such books into Bulgaria. Or, as the interpreter explained: 'The Englishman says it will not get him into trouble to send these books, but thinks it might get you into trouble to receive them.'

The light of a grey dawn filtered into the compartment. 'England is a very small country,' began our Bulgarian again, as if in a last-ditch attempt to resolve all the mysteries of the capitalist world before we reached Venice. 'How does she make enough food for her people?'

I said she had many industries. 'But where does she get

her raw materials?' I said many of them came from abroad. 'But you have to pay for them?' 'Yes.' 'But you did not have to pay for them when you had Canada, New Zealand and Australia and South Africa?' But, yes.

A look of bewilderment was followed by an expression of frank disbelief. Communist indoctrination: it was easy to say that after the train unloaded some of its passengers at the frontier and our Bulgarian friends went off to join the rest of their party in another carriage. But as he shook hands with us and wished us au revoir it was also not difficult to see that, mingled with the look of genuine regret on our curly-headed Bulgarian's face was the frank suspicion that we had been indoctrinated too.

Oxford Mail 22 October 1960

Harry Pollitt was general secretary of the Communist Party of Great Britain from 1929 to 1956. He died in June 1960. The Daily Worker is now the Morning Star. The celebrated typographer, Allen Hutt, was responsible for its layout. The New Daily was an upstart right wing paper that seems to have vanished without trace. Sir Anthony Eden succeeded Churchill as Tory prime minister in 1955. He was forced to resign in 1957 as a result of a bungled attempt to recapture the Suez Canal from Egypt after President Nasser nationalised it in 1956.

7 – I meet my wife

HT was a great admirer of my reporting skills. It was me he deputed to supply the front page highlights at the Oxford Roads Inquiry, the ill-fated scheme to put a road across Christ Church Meadow to relieve the city's traffic gridlock. He was less happy about my role as theatre critic.

What he called my Olympian views were fine for the Oxford Playhouse, where Frank Hauser and the Meadow Players' upmarket programme led to several West End transfers and I often rubbed shoulders with national critics. They led to complaints from the New Theatre and HT tended to take their side. I twice came near to leaving before he did to become assistant editor at the Guardian in September 1961.

In August that year I had a car accident and spent six weeks in plaster from neck to waist with an increasingly maddening itch I could not scratch.

I had just returned to the office and was struggling to decipher a feature which had remained in my notebook since the crash. The firm's only woman photographer, Penny Tautz, dropped by my desk to introduce me to the new darkroom assistant, a dazzling blonde with blue eyes. At the informal editorial booze-up which followed HT's leaving party at Oxford Town Hall a week later she somehow ended up sitting in my lap. We had become an item.

Susan Macfarlane was a Witney girl nearly four years my junior. At the Girls Oxford High School, she was a contemporary of Maggie Smith and Miriam Margolyes and loathed its insistence on academic excellence as much as they did. Since leaving at sixteen, she had become a skilled photographer. For the last two years she had been continuity and script girl at Oxford Film Productions until her boss over-reached himself and the firm went bust.

She had set her heart on succeeding Penny, a good photographer herself on her day but a rather mercurial character. As a result, the chief photographer, Peter Hewitt, swore he would never employ another woman, so Sue left too and took a job at Butlin's as the Bognor Regis holiday camp's first colour operator, then became the Witney Gazette's only photographer apart from the proprietor, Ray Cripps.

Thanks to the growing importance of RAF Brize Norton as a military air base it was a rewarding job and by the time Oxford and County Newspapers took over the independent weekly and her with it, she was already supplying them – and occasionally the nationals – with pictures.

She quickly developed a reputation for reliability and a flair for the offbeat. In the summer months when the diary was slack, Jim Griffiths who had succeeded Peter as chief photographer, would give her a roving commission and could rely on her to come back with a stunning picture, sometimes more than one.

Keith Huyton, the Mail's deputy chief sub-editor, whose job it was to go through the overnight basket, would snaffle any picture of hers that took his fancy and tuck it away in his drawer, so he could splash it on the front-page on Saturday when he was responsible for laying out the paper.

The continuing question about our relationship remained unanswered until 1969, as I remembered twenty-five years later, when perhaps fittingly I recalled the occasion in the Witney Gazette.

Nuptials Chapman style

On December 13 my wife and I celebrate our twenty-fifth wedding anniversary, or rather fail to celebrate. Sue says it's too near Christmas to inflict another party on our friends and relatives, so we're postponing our celebrations until the New Year. At least this year we've remembered. Usually, it is only when my ma-in-law rings up to congratulate us we realise with a guilty start what day it is.

Our lackadaisical approach to a date in the calendar most of our friends mark with bouquets of flowers, candlelit dinners, occasionally even weekend trips to Paris, reflects our haphazard courtship and distinctly unorthodox wedding.

When we first met in 1961 colleagues at Newspaper House thought it the perfect office romance, but as time went by and the *Oxford Mail's* ungainly theatre critic failed to wed the blonde, blue-eyed darkroom assistant they lost interest.

I launched the Anthony Wood Column. Sue became our photographer in West Oxfordshire. Our careers made progress. Our relationship bumbled along fitfully until late in 1969 the realisation that one and one were about to make three finally forced us to regularise it.

On a crisp Saturday morning we marched up Witney High Street to the Register Office in Welch Way with a carrier bag full of clinking champagne glasses, then adjourned to the *Witney Gazette* offices in Market Square to hold our reception.

The first most of our colleagues knew about it was on the Monday morning when the chief photographer Jim Griffiths dropped the pictures and my story in the copy basket. I claim to be the only journalist in Oxfordshire to have written his own wedding report.

We returned from a seven-day honeymoon in Tenerife to pitch into the frenzied round of newspaper activity that marked the run-up to the Yuletide festivities. Our suitcases remained where we had shoved them under our separate beds. The only room in Sue's tiny house in West End big enough to take a double bed was the perma-frosted attic.

On December 25 we pulled them out to retrieve the presents we'd bought in Puerto de la Cruz and decided we had better do something about the mound of dirty clothing. I could hardly turn up for Christmas dinner with my

On our wedding day (photograph Jim Griffiths)

in-laws at Ramsden in a soiled shirt. Sue certainly wasn't going to face her in-laws on Boxing Day wearing grubby underwear.

'Oh Lord,' I groaned, 'shall I fill the bath?' We didn't yet run to a washing machine. 'No,' said Sue, 'we'll take them to the laundrette.' 'It won't be open,' I said. 'Of course, it will,' she said. 'Nonsense…'

Our first matrimonial argument ended as most have since in my utter humiliation. Not only was the laundrette open, inside was a vision of Christmases to come. A harassed dad was folding up a mountain of freshly laundered washing. For the next two hours we basked in a temperature noticeably higher than that of the little house we had left, wrapping up presents while a battery of machines washed, span and dried our clothing.

'Start how you mean to go on,' my mother used to say. Looking back, I suppose it was not a bad beginning to a happy but never quite conventional marriage.

Witney Gazette 1 December 1994

8 – A change of editor

Upon our return from Tenerife the editor came up to my desk, punched me on the shoulder and said: 'Don, you made my week!' He was HT's successor, Mark Barrington Ward, who began his newspaper career as a trainee at the Guardian, went to Africa in 1955 to launch the Ugandan Argus, upon his return in 1959 joined the Westminster Press and edited the Northern Echo for a year before coming to Oxford in 1961.

From day one I had a much warmer relation with him. He shared my passion for the theatre, unwaveringly supported me as a critic, like HT had high regard for my skills as a straight reporter and descriptive journalist and called on me for a succession of major assignments like Churchill's burial at Bladon and the discovery of Leatherslade Farm where the Great Train Robbers divided their loot.

Leatherslade Farm

All day long they kept coming as if the track to Leatherslade Farm was paved with five-pound notes, not mud, and little boys attached great significance to the tyre marks leading from the roadway to the five-barred gate on which a policeman leant with philosophic patience. Their parents gazed past the cowshed up the hill as if the hedges would part, the winding path, which led to the hidden farm, would iron itself out and all the money in the Bank of England would come rolling down.

But really there was nothing to see except fifty yards of muddy track and the gate and the policeman and the cows and, if you were lucky, Mr John Maris, the £14-a-week herdsman whose tip-off brought the CID to this secluded spot off the main Thame-Bicester Road on the outskirts of the Buckinghamshire village of Oakley on Tuesday. Even on a Sunday he had his work to do.

For hundreds it was a holiday and they came from all over the place on bicycles, in cars, on foot to see where the Great Train Robbers had hidden their loot and, seeing little, they speculated. 'Just think,' they said with awe and just possibly a trace of envy, 'two-and-a-half million pounds went up that track.'

Then the curious drove off to try to catch a glimpse of the farm from the snaking roads, which climb to the village of Brill. Those who had come prepared took out their telescopes and binoculars. Those who were brazen enough asked the policeman if he would let them through. 'It will be a month at least before you can do that,' he told them with a disarming smile.

The majority contented themselves with getting their faces on the telly, much to the chagrin of the BBC newsreel man, who wanted them to look in the direction of the farm, as he told them repeatedly, not the television camera. Still, what did it matter as long as everybody enjoyed themselves?

There were babes in arms, there were toddlers and teenagers sucking ices and lollies – the shop down the road did a roaring trade – there were mothers and fathers, there were grandmas and grandpas. A few like the Gladdys family and their golden retriever, Cindy, from Oakley were actually on the lookout for the missing banknotes. 'If there's any money about, Cindy will find it,' a younger member armed with a beach spade told me.

A middle-aged lady tapped the milk-churn on which I was sitting and asked politely: 'Have you looked inside there?' I had to confess it hadn't occurred to me.

Meanwhile, out of sight, the professionals continued their painstaking search for clues at the farmhouse, a search that will spread today with the help of reinforcements to the adjoining farmland, and every now and then the policeman undid the single loop of string that fastened the gate and let out another vehicle, bearing now a VIP from Scotland Yard bound who knew whither, now a batch of weary detectives, knocking off for a bite to eat at Brill police station.

At 6.30pm I too adjourned to attend evensong at the parish church of St. Mary with its tiny spire and its Norman piers supporting fourteenth century arches and watched the three pretty choir-girls in their blue caps progress from the vestry to the chancel, leading the Rector of Lerwick, the Revd H. Oxley, who had exchanged livings for a month with the Vicar of Oakley, the Revd S. Ashby.

The congregation was small, no more than a couple of dozen, but they sang with the enthusiasm of a hundred and the Rector preached a good sermon, even if it was not the homily on money being the root of all evil I was hoping for.

He took as his text: 'And when he was come near, he beheld the city and wept over it,' from the Gospel of St. Luke. Then each of us contributed our mite to the collection, the Rector gave the blessing and we stepped again into the outside world.

A stone's throw away the call of Mammon was still strong. As the setting sun cast its Midas touch on the fields and hedgerows, I directed yet another motorist to Leatherslade Farm, and even in the gathering dusk people were continuing to roll up so that they would be able to say they saw the place where two-and-a-half million pounds was once hidden, or would have done if it wasn't for the hillside in between.

Oxford Mail 19 August 1963

I returned to the story in 1978 when BW asked me to produce a monthly series of famous front pages for the Anthony Wood Column to mark the Oxford Mail's fiftieth anniversary. It was supposed to culminate in December with a supplement on the paper's history I had been working on throughout the year, but by then we were on strike so it did not appear until January 1979.

One of the biggest stories on our doorstep

It might have come straight out of a Peter Sellers comedy or a Wild West film, said the *Oxford Mail* in an editorial note the day after it happened, but it was far from funny.

To begin with the Great Train Robbery of 8 August 1963 – the eighth in my series of famous front pages to celebrate the *Oxford Mail's* fiftieth anniversary – did provoke that sort of angry, bewildered response. But as the enormity and daring of the robbers in hi-jacking the Glasgow-London mail train and getting away with two-and-a-half million pounds sank in, it was impossible to suppress a reluctant feeling of admiration, and amusement.

The main concern at Newspaper House was to keep abreast of one of the biggest stories that ever happened on our back doorstep. The police were convinced the robbers' hideout must be within a thirty-mile radius of that lonely railway bridge near Linslade in Buckinghamshire from which they threw the sacks of banknotes into a waiting lorry, and that meant probably in our circulation area.

So, when the news of its discovery finally broke on the afternoon of Tuesday 13 August, the then news editor and his deputy, Ralph Brain and Peter Sykes, shot off to Leatherslade Farm at Oakley like a couple of greyhounds who had been chained up for a week without food.

They and reporter Allan Brookes [*a railway enthusiast with an encyclopaedic knowledge of timetables!*] were first on the scene. Overhead the then chief photographer, Peter Hewitt circled in a plane from Kidlington Airport taking aerial pictures of the police activity at the farm.

Back in the office Derick Grigs, [*our film critic*], conducted a skilfully drawn-out interview over the phone with the former owner of Leatherslade, Bernard Rixon, – *he never gave another* – who of course hadn't a clue who the chaps he had sold the farm to a few weeks before really were and was now distinctly worried whether he would get his money.

By an odd coincidence Tom Sheppard, an Oxford man who had since retired to the Isle of Man, had acted as steward on a motorcycle trail which followed the robbers' route from Linslade to Leatherslade only twelve months earlier and, as he told me later, if he had realised his old friend 'Tubby' Rixon had moved, he might have put two and two together earlier. The police might have caught the robbers red-handed and he might have received substantially more than the £3,000 he got for his part in guiding them to the lair.

But I think the odds were against it. One of the problems of the police was the simple physical one of sifting through all the suggestions that came pouring in from the public. It was a day or two before they got round to following up the tip-off of John Maris, the herdsman who eventually received £18,000 for the information he supplied about suspicious movements at the farm.

For a few days the excitement focussed on the Oxford area. There was the lady who handed over the keys of the farm to 'a nice gentleman'. There was the boy who might have recorded the car numbers of the robbers in his notebook. There was the Oxford landlady who put two of them up for the night. There were the fascinating pictures of all the knives and forks, mugs, plates, toilet rolls, tins of food, bedding etc. the police discovered at the farm, which local shop staff wracked their brains in vain to see if they could remember any suspicious characters buying.

Then came the first arrests and the discovery of the first caches of missing money and journalists and police scurried off to other parts of the country. But there is no need for me to go into all that, nor to rehearse the details of the subsequent trial at Aylesbury, nor to recap on the drama that followed afterwards. The publication of the train robbers' own book about the crime earlier this year should mean the main facts are still fresh in your memories.

All these years later people still come to Leatherslade Farm to take a look and still go away disappointed. For visitors are no more welcome now than they were on that first Sunday after the discovery when I positioned myself in the gateway to record their reactions and a middle-aged lady tapped on the milk churn on which I was sitting and asked politely: 'Have you looked inside there?'

Anthony Wood Column *Oxford Mail* 1 August 1978

Oxford through the looking glass

It was the White Rabbit, trotting slowly back up Cornmarket again and looking anxiously about at the teatime traffic as he went, as if he had lost something. The passers-by heard him muttering to himself: 'The Duchess! The Duchess! Oh my dear paws! Oh my fur and whiskers! Oh dear! Oh dear! I shall be too late!'

He took a watch out of his waistcoat pocket, looked at it disbelievingly, shook it sadly, then scurried into the nearest shop, surveyed the array of timepieces with a bewildered air, and thumped on the counter.

There was nothing so very remarkable in that, nor did the manager, Mr E.H. Hewitt, think it so very out of the way to hear the Rabbit say: 'I'm late! I'm late!' so vehemently, though when he thought about it afterwards it did seem a little odd. But for the moment he said politely: 'Can I help you, sir?'

When the Rabbit said agitatedly again: 'I'm late!' he beckoned to an assistant. Raymond Alexander looked at the Rabbit's large, antiquated fob watch and, without a word, dropped it into a convenient wastepaper basket, then produced a brand-new glittering timepiece.

The Rabbit laid it solemnly to his ear, listened intently to the tick and smiled. 'I'm late,' he said happily and, producing his wallet, thrust two crackling five-pound notes into the assistant's hand and, without waiting for his change, departed as agitatedly as he had come, muttering to his new acquisition: 'The Duchess! Oh my dear paws! Oh my fur and whiskers!'

The Duchess was in Christ Church kitchen, shaking a pepper-pot vigorously over a large cauldron, which seemed to be full of soup. 'There's certainly too much pepper in that soup!' Alice said to herself as well as she could for sneezing. There was certainly too much of it in the air, and even the Duchess sneezed occasionally.

'Oh, please mind what you're doing,' cried Alice,

jumping up and down in an agony of terror. 'If everybody minded their own business,' the Duchess retorted in a hoarse growl, 'the world would go round a deal faster than it does. Here, you may shake it for a bit, if you like,' she said, flinging the pot at Alice as she spoke. 'I must go and get ready to play croquet with the Queen,' and she hurried out of the room.

Alice followed. 'You can't think how glad I am to see you again, you dear old thing!' said the Duchess as she tucked her arm affectionately into Alice's and they walked off together towards Carfax.

Alice was very glad to find her in such a pleasant temper, and thought to herself perhaps it was only the pepper that had made her so savage in the kitchen. 'When I am a Duchess,' she said to herself (not in a very hopeful tone though), 'I won't have any pepper in my kitchen at all. Soup does very well without.'

Just then, the White Rabbit came hurrying by and, without one word to the Duchess (for whom he had been looking) said to Alice: 'I shall be too late.' 'For what?' asked Alice with concern. 'For *Alice in Wonderland* at the Play-house on Boxing Day, of course,' said the Rabbit, and he retraced his steps and set off down the High, blinking his pink eyes at the traffic lights as he went.

The Mad Hatter was outside a shop in the High, gazing with rapture through the window at a large astrakhan hat. The Rabbit stopped and looked over his shoulder. 'What day of the month is it?' he said to the Hatter: he had taken his watch out of his pocket and was looking at it uneasily, shaking it every now and then, and holding it to his ear.

The Hatter pondered a little and then said: 'The eight-eenth.' 'Two days wrong!' sighed the Rabbit. 'I told them butter wouldn't suit the works,' and he set off angrily up the Turl. The Hatter returned to his window-gazing. 'Bee-ootiful tea-cosy,' he said, looking with adoration at the astrakhan hat. 'Bee-ootiful brown tea-cosy.'

With apologies to Lewis Carroll

Oxford Mail 22 December 1961

The puff for the Playhouse Christmas show was my idea and I arranged the visits to Christ Church and the shops by members of the cast. Alison Frazer was Alice. Margo Cunningham the Duchess, John Stratton the White Rabbit, Tony Tanner the Mad Hatter.

Twentieth century Christmas story

And it came to pass that I took the road to the Baldons and having parked my car, entered into the Church of St. Peter, Marsh Baldon, and found a multitude of villagers assembled there.

And on the steps of the chancel was what looked like a television set and the announcer said: 'This is the story of the Nativity as it might have happened today, or even tomorrow.' And when the congregation had sung a carol, a Beatnik entered bearing an apple and told the story of the fall of Adam.

Then the church was filled with darkness and, lo, when it was light again, there was Mary, 'not well-off but hard-working and living by prayer and trying to follow God's way'. And the voice of an Angel spoke to her and so it was that she went with her husband, Joseph, to the Black Bull, Marsh Baldon.

But the innkeeper said: 'Sorry, mates, the bar is crowded out for this here election and I've no rooms to let,' so the couple bedded down for the night in the garage and there Mary brought forth her firstborn son and wrapped him in swaddling clothes and laid him in a car tyre.

And in the morning the children came skipping up the street, and the first child said: 'Teacher says there is a little baby born in the garage at the Black Bull.' And the second child said: 'On TV it says it is God's own son what he always promised to send us and he's come to our village.'

Then they danced and sang for joy and while they were dancing there came other visitors, wise men who had learned of the birth from the astronomers' instruments or had seen it foretold in the scientists' experiments, a nuclear physicist, an engineer and a surgeon, and offered gifts, each according to his station.

Now, there were also abiding in that same village a group of famous pop-singers and they too came to see the Holy Child, and sung a song called *Mary's Boy Child*. And such was the power of their minstrelsy that others came to see Him. A farmer, a cook, a postwoman wheeling her bicycle up the aisle, a policeman, who offered his helmet to the Holy Child, a builder, who brought a brick, a motor mechanic, a missionary, a housewife.

And when they were all come, then the Rector of Marsh Baldon, the Revd E.A. Charlewood, too visited the Child and reminded the congregation that it was his job, 'to bring God to Man in the sacraments and the Word, and to bring Man to God in leading his prayer, showing him God's Love and teaching His Word and ways'.

And the congregation gave thanks, and having contributed to the collection in aid of the Church of England's Children's Society, departed. And I left too, marvelling greatly at the sincerity and devotion with which the children of the Baldons Sunday School had presented afresh the Bible story.

Oxford Mail 21 December 1963

Deputy editor Arnold Hadwin said to me: 'Smashing piece, Don. Mind you, I had to rejig the page to get it all in!'

Bouncing into 1984

This flight of fancy was inspired by the news that Ernest Marples, a keen cyclist, had bought a specially modified Mini-Cooper with a boot big enough to take a Moulton folding bicycle to use in town! Another inspiration was the quotation, listed in Cyril Connolly's 1994 anthology, The Quiet Grave: 'Imprisoned in every fat man a thin man is wildly signalling to be let out.'

In every fat car there is a thin car struggling to get out, or there will be if the Transport Minister, Ernest Marples, has his way. Collapsible little cockleshells, knee-high to a parking meter, made of rubber or plastic issuing sedately from under the eaves of every Rolls Royce bonnet, whistling like torpedoes from the underslung nobody's business of every E-type Jaguar, glaring hopefully out like travelsick children through the back windows of every estate car.

I can imagine the scene on Monday morning in 1984 at huge carports, which like Big Brethren will bestride the in-roads to Oxford: the chromium-plated limousines, saloons, tourers and seventy-year-tested honkytonk road-sters crawling in at one end and the little minis and bubble cars bounding out at the other.

Here, somebody's valve will have blown and he will be trying to reinflate the many-bladdered mess under which a tinny two-stroke still pulses like an alcoholic octopus. There, a stout party will be girding on the parts of a do-it-yourself half-ton trucklet like a deep-sea diver preparing to submerge.

There, somebody else will have realised that he has for-gotten to put the motor back after mowing the lawn. And, meanwhile, all those who have tested their tubes at the weekend, repaired a week's wear and tear with a spot of liquid plastic and the odd corset bone, listened to the weather forecast and decided successfully how much ballast to carry, will be converging on the city centre.

Minis mousing up the side-streets, bubble cars gumming up the main roads, and at Carfax there they will all be: bouncing up and down like rubber balls on the white lines in an effort to catch a glimpse of the traffic lights before zooming off to their destinations.

At Queen's Lane, the driver of a rubber minibus will be arguing with an inspector: 'But it *was* a double-decker when we started. It's all those people inside. They've stretched it out of all recognition.' At the Station, the occupants of a rubber police car will be trying to prise out the passenger from a punctured rubber taxi in time to catch the 8.50 to Paddington.

At the Martyrs' Memorial, the firemen will be busy pumping up the flameproof rubber extension ladder of a red rubber fire-engine to remove the traditional receptacle* from the top of the monument. And everywhere little rubber vehicles will be cannoning off rubber street signs and lamp posts as belated motorists with cornflakes round their mouths and egg stains on their waistcoats try to reach their workplaces.

'It's a simple test really,' a driving instructor will be reassuring a rather nervous pupil. 'All the law requires of you is that you know how to unpack and inflate your mini-car within forty seconds, that you can drive with the aid of an aqualung if worn for not less than sixty yards using only your periscope, that you can park sideways in a confined space using right and left flippers, and that you have an intimate knowledge… but of course you will have played bar billiards.'

And out he will go with the poor innocent, bound along like a kangaroo in first gear for a couple of hundred yards

* A tin or china chamber pot, a favourite exploit of student climbers.

then, as the pupil gropes for second gear and hits reverse by mistake, smile benignly and pick himself up from the gutter, saying philosophically for the umpteenth time: 'Oh dear, we seem to have turned inside out.'

But despite more serious accidents like the housewife who will drive her mini into the boot of the wrong car and not be discovered until a month later, the absent-minded professor who will back into a holly bush in Banbury Road, and the unfortunate who will drive over a burst water main and be hurled one hundred feet into the air, the rubber car industry will be booming.

After an early setback when a tester will think he has climbed into a car and driven along supported only by his imagination until he dashes his brains out while attempting an elementary cannon off a traffic bollard, the new transparent polythene model will have gone into production and be extremely popular with all but courting couples.

The Cowley convertible with ninety-degree swivel outboard motor will have attracted customers from all over the world by its unique adaptability for use on land, water and in the air. And the Compressed Rubber Company, with the cooperation of their neighbours Morris Sorbo, will just have perfected the ultimate in mini-motoring: the Sorbo Princess, which fits into any boot or bonnet and can be inflated to any size and moulded like modelling clay into any shape from a hearse to a horsebox.

The plan for a road across Christ Church Meadow will have long since been erased from the agenda of the City Council, the University in Congregation and Parliament as outmoded and unnecessary. Lord Marples will have per-formed a charming little ceremony to mark the fact using a minirubber now preserved at the Ashmolean Museum.

There will be a recession in the footwear industry. Chiropodists will have gone out of business. In fact, the only real threat to the stability of the Government will be a speech made in the Commons by the sitting member for Sittingbourne, Kent, pointing out that the average age of learning to walk has risen in the last ten years from 12.3 to 22.7 and the number of ambulatory incapables by 14.9 per cent.

Those who can walk will organise protest marches from Carfax to Catte Street*. A lot of people will turn out in minicars to watch. The police will arrest a few septuagen-erians for standing up in the road. Then everyone will go home 'to put their feet up' and wonder how they ever came to use such a phrase.

Oxford Mail 13 June 1964

Grappling with gravity

While the puritans have been condemning those who wear topless dresses to the bottomless pit, I have been grappling with gravity: a force I imagine, which should in the long run compensate the manufacturers of foundation garments for any temporary loss of business.

* A distance of less than 100 yards.

It was the report of the address by Professor Fred Hoyle and Dr. Jayant Vishnu Narlikar to the Royal Society sixteen days ago that started me off. Not being of a scientific turn of mind, I had thought until then that the matter had been settled once and for all on that famous occasion, the tercentenary of which we celebrate next year, when Sir Isaac Newton was hit on the head by an apple.

But, no, it seems in 1915 that meddlesome man, Albert Einstein, with his theory of relativity, mucked things up and ever since scientists have been using a reversible formula, which makes it equally possible for apples to fall upwards. In short, thanks to Albert, Sir Isaac might just as well have been struck on the seat of his pants or clipped under the chin with a maggoty windfall.

Well, I'm glad for Sir Isaac's sake that Fred and Jay seem to have sorted that one out, though we can't be too sure. They drew mathematical squiggles all over the board, which not even the Fellows of the Royal Society could understand.

But is it right that a matter as grave as gravity, which affects us all, should be treated in the same cheerful hit and miss fashion as a leaking main in the High Street? For all we know, we might leap out of bed one morning and some interfering boffin has lowered the pressure, and sail through the roof or, to cite the opposite case, lower our leaden feet to the floor and crash through the woodwormed boards to the basement.

Not to mention that in the first instance the earth would have slipped a few hundred miles further from the sun, cooling our morning cups of coffee before we had time to raise them to our frost-bitten lips, and in the latter drawn that much nearer, frying our constitutional new-laid eggs in their jackets.

To be fair, Fred and his mate, if they are right, would seem to have pinned gravity down because, according to them, the world is for ever slung in a sort of invisible cat's cradle of interplanetary pulls and, unless half the universe drops off, it cannot go out of control.

But I would like to be sure. As early as the age of nine a friend and I tried to dig a hole to Australia and, although only a goldfish pond somewhere in Headington remains as a monument to our failure, I have never lost faith in the venture. Hang ideas of a Channel Tunnel. With two Test Matches ruined already by the weather this summer, what we need is a good, dependable tube-line between Lords and Melbourne, and I think we would have it if only we could be sure about gravity.

But we don't want a fleet of streamlined coaches bobbing up and down at the centre of the earth like a yo-yo because of this mysterious force, which pulls just as hard at the feet of the Diggers down under as it tugs at the feet of the Limeys in London. Nor do we want the perpetual rain, which falls on the British Isles, pouring through and submerging the sun-drenched wickets below.

Now that these doubts about gravity have been brought into the open something ought to be done to resolve them and where better than the University of Oxford? Cambridge, after all, began it with Newton. Let us finish it off. But please first somebody give us the money. Though I hate to be blasé about the latest trend in fashion, as everyone in Oxford knows, the University Chest has been bare for years.

Oxford Mail 27 June 1964

Dressing divinely

The first time I opened my eyes during prayers I was punished for my sins by the observation that the clergyman kneeling at the altar had holes in his socks and, if I remember rightly, it so shocked me that I did not follow the time-honoured tradition among choirboys of passing on the good news until it reached the head chorister or was suppressed by a well-aimed box round the ears with the bass behind us's *Hymns Ancient and Modern*.

I shut my eyes tightly and pretended it was not so. Nevertheless, it was and from that day forward religious dignitaries with their heels hanging out of their hosiery kept my thoughts on the ground on numerous occasions when they should have been flying upwards.

Now I notice my interest has spread and this week the House of Commons has been debating the Vesture of Ministers Measure. To heathens and Hottentots like myself, who have not kept pace with what the well-dressed vicar is wearing – in fact thought he did very nicely thank-you by having first pick at the annual church jumble sale – the Bill must have come as a surprise.

But up it popped like a piece of burnt toast in the Lords the other week. Between the committee stage of the Protection of Birds Act 1954 (Amendment) Bill and the second reading of the Malicious Damage Bill, the worthy peers spent four hours squabbling over it before passing it by 86 votes to 15, and the unseemly Commons have now approved it by 205 votes to 23.

Therefore, I thought it was worth investigating and to my horror I discovered it has nothing to do with the fact that for the umpteenth year in succession not even the Archbishop of Canterbury is among Britain's Ten Best Dressed Men, but concerns those service items of ecclesiastical over-wear: the chasuble, the cope, the alb and the amice.

Under the judgment of the Judicial Committee of the Privy Council in 1877 it seems all are illegal with the exception of the cope at Holy Communion in cathedrals and collegiate churches, and the clergy should lead the worship of their flocks, though not all do, dressed only in surplices and cassocks.

Thus, the Vestments Measure has been introduced to enable the good ministers to wear anything they please in church subject to the approval of the parish or parochial church council with the Bishop as long-stop in case of an argument.

Low churchmen have waxed hot under their dog collars, interpreting it as step towards Popery, and high churchmen have blushed scarlet behind their amices, citing *The Book of Common Prayer* (which appears to enjoin the use of the full outfit) and saying just the opposite.

People like me with open-necked shirts have secretly come to the conclusion... but let one of the peers speak and let it be Viscount Brentwood. For he said it was the greatest act of appeasement which had taken place since Munich and one appreciates the passion of his point of view.

Why should the worthy Archbishop of Canterbury, kindly soul that he is, have to adapt himself, as he told the House he did, to the vesture used in the various churches out of concern for the feelings and consciences of lay people? Imagine the poor chap freezing to death in a surplice and cassock in one of the lowest of the low churches on Christmas Day, then sweating it out in alb, cope and amice amid the candles the Sunday after in the highest of the high, not to mention the inconvenience of having to do an archepiscopal quick change on his more hectic pilgrimages.

On the other hand, why not? For it is only matter of time before we have colour television and then we shall expect the full pageantry and look forward to the different colours in their seasons: the violet for Lent, the red for Whitsun, the green for Trinity, the white for feasts and the black for All Souls Day and funerals.

Before we become too involved in these and other considerations, however, we had better establish a few basic facts. For a start I should like to see the opinion pollsters conducting surveys to find out just how many people know what an amice and an alb and a chasuble and a cope and a surplice are. I'll bet you not half the church-going population know, let alone the pagan majority.

A cope I said correctly was a sort of embroidered tea-cosy worn round the shoulders, a stole I knew was a long

119

scarf, and an alb I guessed was a bottomless surplice, but a chasuble I regret to say I thought was some sort of Victorian tea-trolley and I hadn't a clue what an orphrey or a maniple were.

Oh yes, I've found out now and I suppose I could tell you. But I suggest you ask your minister, your MP, or any lord you can lay your hands on. After all, that way you will find out what they think about the measure.

In the meantime, maybe parochial church councils ought to start considering what their attitude is going to be with the really with-it clergyman who sees in the measure an opportunity to strike out in a different way. Beat services are commonplace. What about Rolling Stone haircuts?

Doubtless they would be resisted under their own name, but what if the good minister drew support for his long locks from the prophets of the Old Testament or, sporting an extra-long cope, cited Joseph's coat of many colours? Indeed, the Bishop might eventually find himself adjudicating on such inspired creations of ecclesiastical haute couture as the two-piece chasuble, the cutaway alb and the topless surplice.

Only one thing seems certain in this world of change. The cassock will remain the church's foundation garment. It hides everything even, as many a choirboy will tell you, who has just made evensong after an afternoon on the river, his bathing trunks, not to mention the humble civvies the parson's pittance forces most clergymen to dress in off duty.

Oxford Mail 1 August 1964

Pity the poor porpoise

Pity the poor porpoise. I had hoped to make his acquaintance one day when I was old and gross and rich. Sitting on the deck of an ocean-going liner, a panama hat on my head to stop my toupee blowing overboard, a pair of Bermuda shorts on my backside to hide my elastic combinations* and knobbly knees.

I would have raised a flabby arm in salute and he would have honked languorously in reply. Then we would both have gone back to our fishing: he happy in the knowledge that my depredations of the deep would amount to no more than the whiting, upon whose tail he had been treading all morning, I satisfied that, at last, I had met with the most affable of the saltwater mammals.

But, pity the poor porpoise. It is not to be. He has been called up by the United States Navy, which shatters my dreams like a bugler's reveille. Let us call him Keiki, the horrible appellation used by infants to describe everything from Dundee to Madeira, for that is what the Americans have called him, not Percival or Ponsonby, Keiki.

Keiki is at this moment submerged in a pen at the University of Hawaii's Coconut Island Laboratory under the tutelage of Kenneth Norris, Professor of Zoology at Cali-

* Combinations, a long-sleeved vest and pantaloon with a buttoned flap at the back to enable wearers to perform their sanitary functions without taking them off, first made their appearance in the 1870s and remained popular until domestic central heating and man-made fabrics rendered them redundant. They were a frequent source of music hall jokes.

fornia University. He is learning to swim. Oh, don't get the good professor wrong: not swim in the sense you and I mean swim, one foot on the bottom, one hand on the rail, and ready to give up the minute the water comes over our navels.

Swim in a straight line 200ft at a time after an electric kipper, like a greyhound after a hare, so that the United States Navy can improve its knowledge of underwater ballistics. Wherefore, after spending a few weeks flipping up and down his pen for the piscatorial equivalent of peanuts, Keiki will be taken out to sea in his cage and released.

And, if he doesn't do a disappearing act like the Great Train robber Charles Wilson into the wide blue yonder, the television cameras will start whirring, the egg-timers will start timing and Keiki will make a 300-yard sprint for a succulent morsel of smoked salmon.

The films will be developed. The results will look like mouldy ship's biscuits if the moon shots are anything to go by. The Press will hail a success. The boffins will hush up a private failure. Keiki will make a triumphant tour of the world's zoos and, meanwhile back at the Coconut Island Laboratory Sweetie, Bicky, Gripe Water and Nappy Rash the Second will be down under making smart 200ft shuftis after unsavoury mackerel in an effort to salvage the experiment.

But maybe I ought to tell you something about it in particular and porpoises in general. Nice creatures, porpoises, so far as I can make out. Of course, I don't know whether they honk. I made that bit up. But they are friendly and the dramatists make frequent references to the forethought they show to sailors in forecasting bad weather.

Like my dear namesake, George Chapman, in his epic, *Eastward Ho*: 'A porpoise, which is always the messenger of tempests,' or the unkind John Webster, in *The Duchess of Malfi*: 'That cardinal lifts up's nose like a foul porpoise before a storm.' In a word, they are sober and gentle as churchmen and they even look like them with their black or dark grey backs and their flippers folded across their white surplice-like bellies.

But I must not overindulge my flight of fancy. The encyclopaedia, a more reliable guide, says they resemble small whales, have three or four hairs when young, which they lose when they grow up, between eighty to one hundred teeth, which they keep all their lives, and grow from a length of four to six feet.

Moreover, from the soft fat of their heads and jaws is extracted the invaluable porpoise oil, which does not gum or thicken by oxidation, can withstand exposure to very low temperatures without freezing or starting to congeal, does not corrode metal, and is therefore probably lubricating your clocks and watches at this very moment.

But the United States Navy is not interested in that. It wants to know how fast porpoises can swim and for the very good reason that while tame ones have never exceeded nineteen knots, wild ones have kept up with destroyers doing thirty.

They've never passed them you understand. That would be showing off. The porpoises are modest creatures. But they haven't exactly puffed and panted like the poor devils in the boiler room: 'I'll give the captain bleeding porpoises!' For that reason Professor Norris and the Navy have thought up their own method of extracting the porpoise's secret.

The tension is building up as the great day draws near and forecasts of Keiki's speed over 300 yards range from eighteen to eighty knots. In fact, they say, no sporting event has aroused such interest in Honolulu since the days in the nineteenth century when New Zealand missionaries put a stop to surfboard riding because they were shocked to find Hawaiians betting their shirts on the outcome.

Which would be a happy note on which to end except that I forgot to tell you the Americans also hope to find out from Keiki why torpedoes leave no wake. Then they will construct a torpedo, which will fly through the water at anything from eighteen to eighty knots without leaving a telltale chart of its progress for the target vessel to spot. As I said, pity the poor porpoise. Then one day when your ship is about to go down off one of the world's trouble spots, perhaps he'll pity you.

Oxford Mail 15 August 1964

Television coverage poses a political question

With ill-concealed glee I have heard the news that the party leaders may not be able to take their seats after the General Election and suddenly I am on the edge of an opinion poll. At last, there is an issue that catches me by the hair roots and will carry me screaming to the polling station on October 15.

Unpolitical animal that I am, I am looking forward to the moment when the Queen summons a confident Sir Alec Douglas Home, a happy Harold Wilson or a flabbergasted Jo Grimond to her presence and some officious legal body taps them on the shoulder, smiles, and says: 'Just a minute, please, sir.'

Then will come one of those convoluted, old-fashioned, horsehair stuffed incantations beloved of lawyers: 'Under the Representation of the People Act I charge you with securing an unfair advantage for yourself over your opponents in the General Election of 1964 in that you did on divers occasions while standing as a candidate for Kinloss and West, Huyton in Lancashire or Orkney and Zetland broadcast your person and opinions through a medium of propaganda not available to the said opponents, namely a television set.'

The leader will look suitably glum and the legal body will say: 'Dreadfully sorry, sir, if you'll step this way...' Such is the eccentricity of the English Constitution that, leaders of the Conservative, Labour and Liberal Parties though they may be to you and me, to the people who put them where they are – the voters of Kinloss and West, Huyton, Orkney and Zetland – legally they are just potential MPs. So, in the process of gaining their seats, they may have no right to poke their noses between the television knobs on the family hearthrug while their rivals are stamping their feet on the front doorstep or yoohooing themselves hoarse through the letterbox.

Jo will probably be all right. In his constituency most

people haven't got television sets and those that have only switch them on when they want a new tweed pattern. There are no recognisable programmes. To provide good reception up there the BBC would need the television equivalent of Radio Caroline and Richard Dimbleby as ballast.

But Sir Alec and Harold are in a bit of a legal cleft stick. I suppose Harold might just argue that the proximity of Huyton to Liverpool brings it within the interference belt of the electric guitars, which turn the square boxes of that area into Hit Parade seismographs from dusk till dawn.

But he would find it a bit difficult to pursue that argument very far when one of his opponents is Screaming Lord Sutch and once the teenagers of today are the electorate of tomorrow it would be tantamount to surrendering his seat to his rival at the next general election, presuming of course the pop singer intends to give up his peerage.

I have been looking for a way out of Sir Alec and Harold's predicament and, though no immediate solution occurs to me, I offer the following suggestions in the confident knowledge that they will all be quite useless to them.

They could, for instance, arrange for the BBC to substitute some topical series in their constituencies during the election broadcasts like Whizzlestop or Downing Street Ten, but then I feel everyone else would want to see them too.

They could ask the Central Electricity Generating Board to arrange some private and peculiar fault or power failure in Huyton and Kinloss whenever they were on, but then they wouldn't be very popular with the ordinary consumers, not to mention the guitarists, and in any case wouldn't prevent their message reaching postal voters.

Years ago, it wouldn't have mattered. Nobody would have bothered if it meant the price of a postage stamp. But today thanks to the football pools people have been putting crosses on bits of paper and bunging them in the post. In fact, I sometimes wonder what the Returning Officer does with all their postal orders.

So my only proposal that really bears a second thought is the proposition that their opponents be given time to air their views on television too. At the moment, and these are early days yet, it would mean giving another five people a bash on the small screen, but I'm inclined to think it might be worth it.

After all, one of Sir Alec's opponents is that splendid Communist, the Scots poet Hugh McDiarmid, and he has just launched a full-blooded attack on the worthy Member for Kinloss for the 'huge racket of sheep-subsidies'. But there are snags.

If Sir Alec's Scottish Nationalist opponent were seen on television, then we should have to have a Welsh Nationalist as well, and if we had a Welsh Nationalist, then we should have to have an Irish Nationalist or whatever they call themselves. So that before we knew where we were we would have every candidate in the election queuing up at Shepherd's Bush, making a brief shufti in front of the television cameras, waving to the electors back home, then moving off again.

We shall just have to let things take their course, and when a case is brought against Sir Alec or Harold, and when and if they are disbarred from standing for Parliament for five years, as I understand is the penalty under the Representation of the People Act, we shall have to do something about it. Funny Don't Know that I am though, I can't for the life of me think what.

Oxford Mail 26 September 1964

In fact, far from being a don't know I was and would remain a lifelong Liberal!

Sleuthing Scandinavian style

Scandinavian TV detective dramas are now all the rage. When I filed this Personal View from Sweden in 1964 it was a British series that kept us glued to our television screens.

Somewhere in the dossiers of the Swedish police in a township of some 75,000 people on the shores of Lake Hjälmaren about 200 kilometres west of Stockholm there is possibly now a slim file devoted to me: an unusual file, a satisfying file both for the Orebro CID and for me, but one I hope that will not get any fatter in the next fortnight.

No, I haven't been sunbathing with the wrong collar button undone in this country of sun worshippers and got myself arrested for indecent exposure, that seemingly common fate of English tourists abroad. As I write, the sky is blue, the sun is golden, but after a succession of sharp morning frosts have stripped the leaves from most trees but the ubiquitous conifers, the day you can imagine is not exactly warm. Nor have I been caught smuggling cigarettes, whisky or liquorice allsorts, a class of sweets the Swedes go dotty over, into the country. Nor have I… but perhaps I had better start at the beginning.

Friday week was one of those dull, dozy days when the wind, if it should get off its knees, looked to stand fair for Scandinavia, and I said to my cabin-mate as we set off on the Harwich-Esberg crossing with knowledgeable sang-froid: 'Ah well, I think it's safe to eat.' It was. The North Sea even gave us time to follow our coffee with an injudicious beer before it began its indecent game of catch-as-catch-can with the stabilisers of the excellent 10,000-ton Danish Motor Vessel, *England*.

Two hours out at sea, the waves were slapping against the porthole with nauseating inexhaustibility and I was slurping with similar monotony into a jug, whose exquisite design will I am sure bring a blush of shame to my cheeks whenever I extol the grace of Scandinavian metalware here-after.

It was a paler and warier traveller who stepped down the gangplank the other side, passed swiftly through customs – I was too ill even to stagger to the duty-free shop aboard ship and make my brief assault on the British economy – and sank into a thankfully reserved seat in the train to Copenhagen.

The loss of my *Guardian*, I think, and my unfinished crossword first made me feel sometime later that all was not well with me in the state of Denmark, and with that sixth sense I have for smelling calamity I searched my baggage: passport, yes, tickets, yes, money, yes.

Then the awful thought struck me: where was the letter with the address I was making for? I can only assume now at the bottom of the North Sea with the rest of the garbage from the *M.V. England*, though how I came to lose it I can only guess. Most of what happened that night is a sickly blur.

Still, that was only of secondary importance then. My principal reason for visiting Sweden and the only reason for visiting Orebro was to see my old friend, Chris Prior, recently arrived there, whom many Oxford people knew, and I would look a fool if I returned without setting eyes on him.

Vainly I argued with myself he was bound to meet me at the station, a certainty that became less and less sure as I made my muddled way along the Saturday night and Sunday morning of the Swedish railway system, and even if he didn't, I convinced myself, the local police kept a list of aliens. So it was, some five or six hours behind schedule, I presented myself at that favourite television series, *Z-Cars*, New Town police station's equivalent in Orebro, and was greeted by an affable sergeant.

Through a police cadet who could speak English he told me, after inspecting my credentials with some sympathy, that he was very sorry. Not even their counterpart to Chief Inspector Barlow could disclose an address on the aliens list. But he would see what else he could do, and that turned out to be one of the finest examples of international goodwill it has been my good fortune to encounter.

The case was passed to the John Watt of the force, who having gleaned as much vital information as he could from me in broken English, set to work with a telephone. Truth to tell, he was rather too smooth and well turned out for John Watt. You might say he was a John Watt who had served a year or two under Simenon's famous fictional French detective, Le Patron, and he seemed to have acquired some of Maigret's uncanny insight into human nature. His patience and politeness were staggering. He even asked my permission before he lit a small cigar in his own office, having discovered I no longer smoked.

Then, after about twenty vain phone calls to the homes of various school and college heads, he escorted me to his new, shiny black Volkswagen and we beetled off, seemingly to round up the entire English-speaking population of Orebro. Chris is a teacher of English there.

Most of them live apparently amid the muddy, as yet unmade up roads of a vast new suburb of luxury flats. Anyway, it was there with the help of frequent radio contact with headquarters in the best *Z-Cars* tradition that John Watt at last found someone who had heard of Chris: a young Yorkshireman with a Swedish wife. Then with a shake of the hand and a quick discounter of my professions of gratitude he abandoned me, as I thought, to my fellow countryman and his wife and they nobly continued the search, the man trying to piece together the fragmentary memories of his one recent meeting with Chris, his wife making further telephone calls, until eventually we gave the whole thing up for the time being and went out to look at the view above Orebro.

Not so, our detective though, I had misjudged him. In the mean-time he had found Chris and was busily touring the city with him looking for us, and so it was that after a final telephone call on our return to the couple's home I was at last delivered to his doorstep only six hours after I had arrived in Orebro, which I think is pretty good service.

Oh, I know you could say the detective could have saved himself a lot of trouble by cheating and looking at the aliens list in the first place. He says in fact he had a call from someone we had phoned earlier who supplied the information. But I admire a man who plays the game by the rules.

Personal View from Sweden *Oxford Mail* 31 October 1964

Z-Cars was a gritty television drama which followed the work of the police force in the fictional town of Newtown in the North of England from January 2, 1962 to September 1978.

No flies on me

So, there I was, a foreign body in an alien country, with my zipper in my hands and my trousers round my ankles, and a pretty fix I might have been in if it hadn't happened in a Stockholm bedroom.

Oh, don't worry madam. I upheld British dignity. Two anxious minutes with a pair of nail-clippers, a prayer from the heart to the Lord of the Flies and a few tentative promenades along the carpet like a catwalk mannequin and I was all right. But just you think what might have happened.

There I was with my nearest spare pair of trousers hanging in a wardrobe the other side of the North Sea and there was my landlady likely to burst in, crying: 'Mistair Shapman, may I come in?' at any minute. It still brings the sweat to my brow when I think about it.

Supposing, I said to myself, as I rummaged in my duffel bag for my clippers, if I bolt my door and keep my mouth shut. Ridiculous! Being a Swede, she'll think I'm committing suicide. Well, supposing, I thought as I prised open the fastener, I take the bull by the horns, appear in my pants, waving aloft my trousers, and with elaborate pantomime explain the calamity that has befallen me. Absolutely out of the question! Ten to one she'll think I'm making advances to her.

Well then, supposing – bang, bang, bang with the heel of my shoe: get in, you little devil – I… But just then the zip fastening slid forward with a happy chuckle, the teeth closed upon one another like a little boy's fingers, and thankfully I girded my loins.

All right, you don't need to tell me. I fully realise my foolhardiness now. I shouldn't have gone out of the country without buttons.

It wasn't as if I hadn't been warned. There was that occasion when I was working in the north of England. One morning I marched down three flights of stairs three times from my bedroom to the cellar, did a hasty repair and marched up again only for my trousers to fail to remain upstanding. On that occasion I remember committing irreparable havoc with a chisel and a mallet. I had to boot-polish my shirttail before going to the office in a pair of charcoal greys that had seen better days.

But, personal tribulations apart, is it right that the man-ufacturers of male attire should persist in fitting our cod-pieces with these shoddy by-products of sartorial ingenu-ity? I know, ladies, you will say: 'What's wrong with but-tons?' and since you usually have to sew them on when they come off, you have a right to ask the question.

But it's like high heels, which make holes in the lino-leum, get stuck in gratings and snap off at awkward moments. Some men prefer zips: you see, they don't need so much doing up.

Purely in the interest of science I have this week been conducting an experiment, and I find that on average the man with a zip can stay in bed thirty-one seconds longer than the man with buttons. On Tuesday the difference was actually fifty-four seconds, but I think that's pushing it a bit. In my enthusiasm to improve on my time I got my feet caught in my braces on Thursday and practically catapul-ted myself into the wardrobe.

So, take it gently, fellow zippers. While I don't for one minute believe that any of the dire accidents that were pre-dicted when zips were first introduced in trousers could really happen, there are minor perils attached to their func-tioning, particularly for the corpulent.

Dons still sometimes regale themselves with the story of the fat Fellow who, during a sumptuous repast, slid down his zip a few notches to make room for more. At the end of the meal, he was somewhat alarmed by the struggle he had to do it up again. But not nearly as alarmed as when he rose and, the edge of the tablecloth being firmly attached to him, trailed after him the college's best silver.

I myself witnessed the sad case of the gala first night when a lady sweeping down the aisle in a lace evening gown became momentarily attached to a gentleman in a relaxed evening suit, the flimsy fabric snagged in the protruding teeth, there was a loud sound of ripping and the gentleman suddenly found himself sporting an extra shirt-tail.

But it is not fates such as these, I fear. It is the dread that one day a delayed action defaulting zip will leave me standing at Carfax in the centre of Oxford – with my trousers down.

Oxford Mail 21 November 1964

Ever-squeezer Scrooge

Am I thrifty or am I just mean? I have this debate with myself every time I come to the end of a toothpaste tube. I am one of those people who cannot bear to discard a container until I am sure it's empty.

It is a standing joke in our house that I will go on squeezing droplets of white paste onto my brush long after everybody else has given up and moved on to a new tube. I perform similar wonders with the brushless shaving cream

– an altogether trickier operation because it involves applying pressure with both hands until the soap reluctantly dribbles out of the nozzle, then catching it in the palm of my hand before it drops into the washbasin or, worse, on the floor.

I scrape away at marmalade jars, cursing the short-sightedness of manufacturers for making them with kinks in the neck. I stand sauce bottles on their sides and on their heads to encourage them to surrender their last oozings. I have even been known to turn my attention to the cat's Whiskas, though that usually squelches from the tin in a satisfying dollop thanks to the jelly in which it is encased.

We did once have an ingenious plastic device like a miniature mangle that worked well until I snapped the hands applying too much pressure to a particularly obstinate toothpaste tube. My wife, Sue, has her own simple but effective method for dealing with tubes of moisturising cream. When they no longer respond to her fingers, she cuts them in half and seals them with clingfilm and a Bulldog clip. The cream trapped inside usually lasts another couple of weeks.

But why can't the manufacturers devise containers that surrender their contents without a struggle? Why don't they devote as much energy to developing user friendly packaging as they do to making sure their goods catch your eye in the supermarket? Or do they think it's in their interest for us to be wasteful?

By accident I attended an international packaging congress at Gothenburg in 1964. I was visiting my friend in Sweden and decided I ought to take a look at the country's second city and biggest seaport before I came home.

I arrived at the tourist information centre to discover every room in the place had been booked by delegates to the conference. The nearest B&B that could accommodate me was twenty miles away and was inaccessible by bus or train. A delegate who was overnighting there himself took pity on me and gave me a lift in his car, so when next morning he insisted on showing me round the exhibition it would have been churlish to refuse.

Most of the stands displayed products that were mind-bogglingly boring – machines that produced crushproof soap flake packets, plastics that withstood unbelievably high or low temperatures, labelling dyes that would not poison toddlers who preferred the containers to the contents. But one my newfound friend singled out with pride.

Within two years, he predicted, it would have completely revolutionised our approach to cleaning teeth. I would see it in bathrooms all over the world. It looked like any other toothpaste tube except it had a plastic hook on the bottom so that you could hang it up in the rack with your toothbrush. 'Such a simple idea,' he said. 'So clever!'

After my return to England, I kept a lookout for the new toothpaste container. I decided I would have to buy one even if it meant abandoning my regular Colgate for Macleans or Pepsodent. The months lengthened into years and, in the end, I came to the conclusion my Swedish friend was wrong. There was some hang-up with the hang-up toothpaste tube he had failed to envisage.

A couple of Christmases ago I found out what it was. A friend gave one of my daughters a tube of pineapple and strawberry bath gel as a present. It had a plastic hook on the end so it would hang from the towel rail. After a few weeks I realised I was emerging from my morning bath smelling distinctly fruity. You've guessed... If you didn't shut it properly, the push-button dispenser in the cap leaked. By the morning there was a small but pungent bead of soapy jam in the bottom of the bath.

Unlike Archimedes, I didn't leap out yelling: 'Eureka!' I lay there in the sickly-scented suds imagining Swedish scientists battling vainly to prevent toothpaste oozing in long white ribbons from inverted tubes. Gravity feed! When you think about, finding a way of turning it off that didn't cost the earth might be the answer: the tube that gave its all to the last squeeze.

Really though, I suspect the manufacturers would rather you got tired, stopped squeezing and bought another one.

Witney Gazette 13 April 1995

9 – Alias Anthony Wood

For the third time in my career head office intervened. Towards the end of 1964 BW received a directive from London to brighten up the leader page and introduced the Anthony Wood Column to replace the ragbag of gossip notes, Mail Diary.

He had been tickled by an item I wrote for that, suggesting a doll that had just gone on sale in souvenir shops of the former Tory premier Harold Macmillan in his robes as the latest Chancellor of Oxford University would be 'useful for Labour supporters to stick their pins in!' and asked me to write it.

The then still somewhat novel conversational tone I adopted, already a mainstay of radio and television programmes, encouraged readers to write in or phone me, and my readiness to write about anything that interested them led to some remarkable stories.

The celebrated seventeenth century Oxford antiquary, Anthony à Wood, from whom I took my name was compiling his diaries in the shadow of the Civil Wars and few shared his passion for the past. I was more fortunate. Memories of the Second World War were beginning to fade.

My burrowing in the archives reflected a popular mood and it helped that I could rely on the input of experts like Raphael Samuel, who ran the oral history workshop at Ruskin College, and Malcolm Graham, head of Oxfordshire Studies at the City Library in Westgate.

Anthony Wood became a character whose interests reflected those of my readers rather than mine. In addition to delving into local history thanks to them at different times I enthused about anything and everything.

By the time Britain and Oxfordshire's postwar prosperity forced Oxford and County Newspapers to move from traffic-clogged central Oxford in 1972 my column had become one of the most eagerly read features in the Oxford Mail. Meanwhile, my offbeat musings under my own name continued.

God-forsaken

Colin Dick tells me he heard so much about river gods in his childhood that he always half-hoped, half-dreaded he would meet one. Psychologists therefore, will not be surprised to find that wish-fulfilment expressed in the exhibition of *Thames Motifs* he had in the Long Gallery of Abingdon Abbey during the Vale of the White Horse Festival.

From more than one of his canvases, portly gentlemen in their birthday suits glared balefully out with that malevolent look on their faces that you sometimes catch the hoarier denizens of Parson's Pleasure, the nude male bathing place on the River Cherwell, giving you when you pass through in a punt.

Maybe he didn't intend them to be unfriendly. That's just the way they appeared to me. Minor deities are so much out of fashion these days that I don't imagine them taking very kindly to being dragged out of hiding by a fanciful artist. All the same, I'm glad they're there, leaning on their tridents and, I believe, sitting on their tails because without the occasional reminder that they still exist the world would be in danger of becoming such an impersonal place.

The Scandinavians may still keep up their trolls. Indeed, they've turned their effigies to considerable commercial advantage, but what do the rest of us do towards preserving the image of the lesser gods? Once a year we insert an advertisement in the Situations Vacant column. You know the one: 'Father Christmas wanted for busy department store, end of November to the middle of January. Must be firm with children. Apply Box…'

That dreary festive gentleman in the red nightshirt with the cotton wool stuffed in his ears and nostrils is all we've got left. The celebrities the Greeks and Romans made such a fuss about have completely disappeared. No Pressed Steel worker snatches the naked Venus from the waves at Clacton. No woman don, punting up the Cherwell, is surprised by Zeus in the shape of a swan. No Amalthea is caught in a Didcot supermarket stuffing her cornucopia full of cat food. No Orpheus enters the Hit Parade at No. Ten.

No Mercury plays for England on the right wing. Only in the world of sport occasionally do the mythological figures persist. Those people who think I'm knocking the accepted religions, which of course I'm not, won't thank me for pointing out that the St. John most people venerate in Liverpool wears football boots. But it's a fact. How else do you explain the lamentation in Brazil except by describing the defeat of their team as the toppling of the contemporary gods of soccer, the crippling of Pele as the humbling of an immortal.

A long time ago when I was reading Ernest Hemingway's novel, *The Old Man and the Sea*, I remember thinking to myself that the baseball stars the ageing fisherman drooled over in his out-of-date newspapers seemed like gods to him because the matches took place so far away. Looking back now, I think that may be the answer. Maybe the world has advanced so far technologically that the ancient gods no longer have enough room to manoeuvre. Maybe they've all emigrated.

Have you noticed how Selene hasn't smiled since the Russians and American landed their rockets on the moon? Maybe she's gone to join her fellows on some more distant planet, and maybe some off-course astronaut will find them all: Vesta ticking off her Virgins for wearing miniskirts, Apollo cursing British Summer Time for making him get up early, Bacchus trying to make vodka out of Soviet rocket fuel, Juno nagging Jupiter as usual.

Of course, I could be wrong. A few years ago, I would have said I was bound to be. But that was before I advanced the facetious theory in a similar column that you could hear how the world began. Only the other day I read two young scientists at the Marconi Institute in America

142

had picked up signals on a very sensitive receiver, which they claimed were the bangs with which creation started. I have learnt it doesn't pay to joke with the beautiful Muse sitting at my elbow… but, hush, I don't want her to emigrate too!

Oxford Mail 23 July 1966

It always rains on Sundays

Back in 1947 an Ealing film company made a melodrama featuring the English weather called *It Always Rains on Sunday*, which is probably by now doing the rounds of the dustier fleapits on the fringes of the Sahara. For all I know in that part of the world it may be bigger box office than *Cleopatra*.

The rain running down the windowpanes, the people scurrying through the streets with raised umbrellas, the water butts welling over may not seem very exciting to us, but they are undoubtedly just the spectacles to bring a look of awe to the unwashed faces of the children of the desert. In fact, I can imagine them rushing home after sitting through two performances to the tent of their patriarch, falling on their knees before his time-ravaged countenance and saying: 'Sire, sire, we have seen a watery wonder.'

He, however, is older and wiser. 'My little ones,' he says gently, running his parched fingers over his wrinkled visage in a vain effort to recollect when his dry chaps last felt the kiss of rainwater. 'My little ones, it is all an illusion, a mirage of the film-makers to make us buy more soft drinks and put up the prices of the water-sellers. Go back to milking the camels and say your prayers to Allah that someday we may find an oil well and conduits may stretch across the desert. Then shall we anoint ourselves with water and our wives will remove the yashmaks from their faces.'

Thus, do those who have lived longer always exercise their privilege of knowing more about the weather than their juniors.

Yet I cannot believe that the hoariest sage, however wizened, would have the temerity to advance a theory as fanciful as that put forward by a mathematician from Durham University in the latest issue of the scientific journal, *Nature*. This worthy gentleman, who I suspect cannot even hide behind the cloak of advancing years, would have us believe there is a calculable strategy for running through rainstorms without getting wet.

What is more, he wants to tax our brains with a formula based on the angle at which the rain is falling and the speed at which we run.

Now, it is all very well for a missionary to explain to a Bedouin that a camel may pass through the eye of a needle, especially when the fount of black liquid has failed to come welling up from the ground in answer to the convert's prayers. But to tell the average Englishman, who always carries an umbrella, a raincoat, a plastic mackintosh, a pair of wellington boots or in the case of certain gentlemen I know rubber galoshes, how to cope with a cloudburst is another matter.

It is not as if this Durham chap contents himself with a

learned treatise on the theory of aerodynamics to be employed in the design of sou'westers for use in a hurricane or an exposé of the danger of a Malacca handle as a conductor of electricity in the event of your umbrella tip being struck by lightning.

If you have the take-off speed of Superman and the rain is coming towards you, he says, you should travel horizontally, presumably stretched out on one of those skateboards with your arms thrashing the pavement like the front legs of a crocodile. If you can't move at all, you should incline your body to the angle of the rain so that is strikes the top of your head and other protuberances, making them infinitely wet but maximising overall dryness.

To which I reply: the fool, the nincompoop, the blithering idiot. Has he carried out any experiments in the field? Has he tested his theories in a good old English shower? Well, I have and I can tell him that far from maximising overall dryness, standing at the angle at which the rain is falling minimises underwear comfort. The drips run down your neck, course down your vest, collect in a pool in the seat of your combinations, then cascade down your legs to be absorbed by your socks.

Not that such possibilities would deter the natives I left grovelling on their faces before their elderly chieftain. If the heavens suddenly broke about their ears, they would be out singing in the rain with Gene Kelly, and with good reason. Shortage of drinking water is a growing world problem. In fact, if Oxfordshire's noted weather prophet, Father William Connick, is right when he predicts there will be a serious drought in the next few years, then we should all be praying with him that somebody finds a cheap way of taking the salt out of sea water. That would raise a cheer, even down the salt mines in Siberia.

Oxford Mail 30 July 1966

Life and death in cold storage

A few years ago, a Cairo travel agency did quite a business offering seat reservations on the first public rocket flight to the moon. Now an American firm is doing just as nicely thank-you keeping bodies in cold storage until the scientists have the answer to their cause of death.

What makes both projects equally appealing to the gullible is that the dreams on which they are floated will probably one day come true. What makes both equally ridiculous is that the smart Alecks marketing them do not possess the monopoly of the scientific developments necessary to carry them out.

I could be wrong. When the travel agency made its offer, I remember to my chagrin working out that if each passenger saved £10 a day, by the time he came to take off on his 239,000-mile journey he might just have enough to pay for his fare.

The firm offering a personal second coming is even more reasonable. Leave us your money, they say, and we will invest it for you: a promise that should induce a great many mommas and poppas to jump out of the incinerator into the freezer.

All the same, I cannot bring myself to believe in their offer to refurbish today's clapped-out bodies for tomorrow's brave new world. Although I am an agnostic, there is something sacrilegious about it that makes me uneasy. Lots of chaps in white coats with blowlamps thawing out the clients one by one, surgeons inserting plastic hearts and polyester kidneys, then lots of Americans in sterilised modesty smocks sitting up. It's all too macabre to be true.

Even if they did it tastefully, you know: piped music, pine scented air, Bibles on the bedside tables with the banknotes, photographs of their great-great-grandchildren, that sort of thing. And it poses too many questions. What will they do about funerals? How will they dispose of the deep-frozen's personal effects? Who will decide whether they are spending their long winter up above or down below?

As soon as I heard about it, I began to have nightmares in which I saw miles and miles of ice blocks laid out on marble slabs, all waiting patiently for the coming of the spring, the thawing of their glacial coffins, and a second lease of life.

Only instead of the moratorium attendants and their blowlamps and the surgeons with their scalpels stepping in when the doors were flung open, a civil servant would appear with a sheaf of papers from the State Bureau of Population. He would say to the directors of the great human cold store as he walked down the frosty corridors, slapping his fur gloved hands together to emphasise his point: 'I'm sorry, gentlemen, but the United States Government just cannot let you bring any of these stiffs back to life. We've had enough trouble on our hands feeding the existing population since that jerk Addams found his death-defying serum. What we need now is a few earthquakes, hurricanes and avalanches to cut numbers down, not an extra quarter-of-a-million creeps from the twentieth century to send them spiralling up.'

Then I would wake up in a cold sweat wondering nervously whether the cooling system had gone wrong and I had melted in the middle of the night, suddenly realise where I was, roll over, go back to sleep, only to dream an even more horrible dream.

The piped music would be playing *Where-ere You Walk*, the scent of pines would be strong, and a shaft of sunlight would be breaking through. On the slab, a sweet old American would be coming back to life. 'And my dear wife?' I would hear him asking the attendant. The attendant, whose face I would suddenly notice had turned unnaturally white, would start blurting out a carefully rehearsed explanation.

'Well, you see it was like this, sir. There was this terrible power cut in 1984, then the cold store operatives who were running the emergency generators went on strike, for extra pay, and your wife being nearer the... Look, I don't want to upset you but...' If only I had forgotten to turn off the electricity before I went away on holiday, if only I hadn't found that packet of soggy peas in the freezing compartment of the fridge when I got back.

Oxford Mail 24 September 1966

Collecting a fortune

Sooner or later, somebody is going to say they have the largest collection of dustbin lids in the world. It is only a matter of time. As the century proceeds and the urge to collect something somebody else doesn't becomes more and more difficult to fulfil, collector's pieces are going to become more and more way out.

Already I curse myself that I didn't keep the cardboard milk-tops I used to flick against the playground wall as a boy, and my father's generation must feel much the same way about the cigarette cards they mishandled in their youth. Today they are things of the past and have a curiosity value. In a few years' time they may be rarities worth hundreds of pounds.

To give you an idea of what I mean, let me cite the example of the late Ian Fleming, creator of James Bond. As a young man he hit upon the notion of collecting first editions of works that were 'milestones of human progress' – Madame Curie's thesis, which told the world she had isolated radium, that sort of thing. Now they are worth a fortune.

I am not saying every collector can hope to be as farsighted or fortunate as that, but even the chap who has cared for his great uncle's pennyfarthing assiduously may suddenly find he's hit upon a second source of income.

When I walked through Christ Church meadows recently during the filming of the Tommy Steele musical, *Half A Sixpence*, it was a revelation. The owners of Edwardian cars, Edwardian boats and Edwardian carriages were all there doing very nicely thank-you out of hiring their vehicles to provide authentic background atmosphere, and from what a genial ostler in charge of two horses, which would later be pulling a coach in the Lord Mayor's Show, told me it would seem, like the best of actors, they were never out of work.

But usefulness in a historical context is not the only criterion of worth. Demand plays its part. If every artist could produce fantastic masterpieces, then paintings by Old Masters would not fetch such high prices. If every collector who wanted one had been able to get one, then the World Cup stamp, which was specially overprinted to mark England's victory, wouldn't already be worth above its face value.

It is anticipating the demand that is so difficult. If we had been born a couple of centuries ago with our present knowledge, we would have filled great depositories with period furniture, silver and china. The trouble is that we were not, and guessing what examples of twentieth century living will be in demand in twenty-first century Britain or America is like trying to forecast the winner of the Grand National.

I am convinced that a collection of early radio and television sets would be a good investment, but who's going to risk their money on a lot of dusty valves and cathode ray tubes? Not me, nor seemingly most other people.

When a friend took his 1929 Morris Cowley into the garage for its test recently, a vehicle incidentally now worth more than when it was new, the proprietor said sadly: 'We didn't know how to get rid of these things fast enough in the 1930s.' Thus, the whirligig of time brings in its revenges.

Yet even though people are less cavalier than they were a hundred or even twenty years ago in their approach to things of the past, even though collecting anything of value has become something of a craze, I have the feeling history will still manage to make fools of us. I can just see that chap with his dustbin lids turning up on the set of some epic about Harold Wilson in the twenty-first century and the director saying: 'Get that fool out of here! What I want is manhole covers, genuine twentieth century manhole covers.' I mean, who is going to collect those?

Oxford Mail 15 October 1966

Thinking inside and outside the box

After staring long and hard at a picture of a man leaning over a woman, the cowboy remarked to the bartender in the film, *The Oxbow Incident*: 'I feel sorry for that guy, always getting there and never doing anything about it.' He was a realist. John Keats was a romantic. Of a similar situation in his *Ode on A Grecian Urn*, he wrote:

Bold lover, never, never canst thou kiss,
Though winning near the goal, yet do not grieve,
She cannot fade, though thou hast not thy kiss.
Forever will thou love and she be fair.

It's remarkable, isn't it, how transparently obvious their diametrically opposed philosophies of life become, simply from the expression of a few well-chosen words on the same pregnant theme. A psychiatrist could not have supplied a more illuminating guide to their characters if he had asked them to voice their innermost thoughts.

Yet, curiously, it is the psychiatrist's probings that frighten us. It is venturing an opinion on an avant-garde play or an abstract work of art that reduces us to quivering jellies. With all the smug arrogance of Alf Garnett we sound off about the rights and wrongs of the Breathalyser Test or the Government's economic cuts, never dreaming the unmistakable image of ourselves we are conjuring up in the eyes of our fellowmen.

My own irrational fear is not that I will reveal myself in conversation to be a bigot or a prude or a prig, but suddenly in some moment of acute embarrassment my skull will become a crystal ball and disclose what is going on in my head. Occasionally I find myself thinking dreadful thoughts about someone, saying to myself 'You stupid idiot!' or things far worse, then suddenly I awake from my daydream and catch him looking at me with an uneasy glint in his eye.

That moment is far more unnerving than remembering out of the blue with a guilty start some unpardonable sin like knotting all the choirboys' surplices together and hanging them over the gravestones in the hope they would give the vicar a heart attack in the gathering dusk.

It makes me bring my hand up to my lips to make sure I haven't said anything, then pass it on up my face to make absolutely certain my forehead hasn't done the dirty on me, started spelling out my evil imaginings in big, bold letters across my brow. To the best of my knowledge so far it never has, and after coming across an article about a forty-seven-year-old former American bellhop in an old issue of *Life Magazine* I happened to be reading the other day I am now coming round to the opinion that maybe it never will.

For the last twelve years Ted Serios has been gazing into the lens of a camera, thinking, pressing the shutter, and producing, not a closeup of his face, but a somewhat fuzzy, out-of-focus, yet recognisable snapshot of his thought. Scientists, suspecting trickery, have stripped him naked, strapped an encephalograph to his head, locked him in a shielded metal chamber and asked him to project his thoughts through heavy panes of lead-impregnated glass.

Yet still the mysterious images have kept appearing on the undeveloped rolls of film and the odd thing is that even Serios himself has not been able to recognise some of them. He has conjured up a building to which he cannot put a name. He has thought of a Greek statue he cannot remember seeing. He has envisaged a scene from a war before he was born.

I used to think it was only a matter of time before psychiatrists working with computers would be able to analyse the working of our conscious and subconscious minds with an accuracy that made a mockery of human thought. Now I am hopefully fanning the embers again of an old reactionary conviction that the human brain will prove to be more devious than the most devious manmade machine.

If, as Ted Serios's snapshots suggest, we have locked away in our craniums not only the miscellaneous experiences of our own transitory lives but hidden in the deeper recesses, in most cases beyond our recall, the whole gamut of creation's animadversions since the beginning of time, maybe the computers will never catch up with us.

Maybe, like the man in the cowboy's picture, they will be always getting there, never doing anything about it. Maybe, like the lover on Keats's urn, we will be able to go on believing that life is fair, that:

Beauty is truth, truth beauty: that is all
Ye know on earth and all ye need to know.

Oxford Mail 20 January 1968

In search of gopher wood

Every time we read the story of the Ark in the Bible, we come across God's command to Noah in verse fourteen of *Genesis*, chapter six: 'Make thee an ark of gopher wood.' But how many of us stop to ask ourselves what gopher wood is?

Neither the translators of the King James version of 1611 did, nor the scholars responsible for the revised version of 1881–5. They simply spelled out the letters of the Hebrew word they found in the manuscript in English. But for the children of Fyfield Primary School that wasn't good enough. They wanted to find out more and, when the obvious sources of information proved unrewarding, they decided to enlist the aid of a chap with a helpful sounding name, Anthony Wood.

'Dear sir,' said the letter Judy Hemming, Janet Whitaker, Rosemary Harris and Lucille Wasley sent me on behalf of their classmates, 'Please have you any information about gopher wood? We phoned all the museums in Oxford and they did not know, nor did the Forestry Commission.'

I got down the *Oxford English Dictionary* and read the definition: 'Gopher: (1611), the tree of the wood of which the ark was made. Chiefly in combination gopher wood applied in the United States to the yellowwood (*cladrastis tinctorial*).' Then I rang the Superintendent of the Oxford Botanic Garden, Kenneth Burras.

'Gopher wood?' he said, sounding puzzled. 'That's a new one on me. We've got an example of the *cladrastis lutea* in the Garden, which was planted here in 1850. That's an American yellowwood and has beautiful yellow leaves in the autumn. But I've never heard it referred to as a gopher tree. Why don't you try the University Department of Forestry?'

I rang the University Department of Forestry and after delving into a lot of books on my behalf they succeeded in finding two more yellowwoods, one which grows in Japan and one which grows in China, but not a mention of gopher wood nor any other wood that might be good for building arks.

Finally, I rang Professor Godfrey Driver, the celebrated Hebrew scholar who received a knighthood in the New Year's Honours List, and at last received an authoritative answer. 'Oh yes,' he said, interrupting his work on translating the *Old Testament* for the *New English Bible*. 'It's rather complicated, but I'll see what I can do,' and sure enough through the post a couple of days later arrived this admirable summary of the experts' deliberations on the subject.

'The most probable view is the wood of the cypress tree (*cypressus sempervirens*) is meant. This is a type, of which the wood has a close and tough texture and which grows in great abundance in the Middle East, being found in the Lebanon and on Mount Hermon, in Assyria and Armenia. It is known to have been used for ships by the Phoenicians, Cretans and Greeks, and also by Alexander the Great. We are therefore putting this in the *New English Bible*, of which we hope to bring out the *Old Testament* in 1970.

'The only other wood that has been suggested is teak, which is now used in Iraq for riverboats, but this is an Indian wood, which is not likely to have been imported into Palestine in the time of the *Old Testament*, especially when cypress was available in large quantities close at hand. It is also not impossible that the Hebrew *gopher* and the Greek *kuparissos* are at bottom the same word.'

Flushed with success, I telephoned Fyfield School and learnt from the teacher in charge of the project, Peter O'Neill, a student from Culham College doing his final teaching practice, that in the meantime the children too had been busy. They had written to the Israeli Embassy in London, receiving a very nice letter in reply from the Ambassador also suggesting cypress wood, and now their headmistress, Mrs G.M. Feeney, was writing to the French archaeologist who claimed to have discovered the remains of the ark on Mount Ararat to see if he could help.

Just to round off the venture I suggested they might like to travel into Oxford and look at the Botanic Garden's example of the yellowwood tree, which is sometimes referred to as the gopher tree in the United States, and the Garden's examples of the cypress, and that's what they did.

Mr Burras, the superintendent, kindly showed them round, and they went away bearing some seed from the Garden's two examples of the *cypressus sempervirens* to grow their own cypress trees and – who knows? – perhaps one day build their own ark!

Anthony Wood Column *Oxford Mail* 16 February 1968

According to Wikipedia, speculation continues about what gopher wood is. Some, noting the physical similarity between the Hebrew letters g (gimel ג}) and k (kaf כ}), suggest that the word may actually be kopher, the Hebrew word meaning pitch, thus kopher wood would be pitched wood: ideal for an ark that had to float!

The Bootleg Gentleman

Like I said, there was this speakeasy in St. Ebbe's called Morrell's Brewery or something, which the buzz had gone round the G-men were going to raid. So the Boss said: 'Hey Tiny,' he said. He always calls me that on account of my size. 'Let's give the place the once over. We can lift a few barrels of the hard stuff and skin the cat over the state

The Bootleg Gentleman (photograph Sue Chapman)

border before the cops have had time to make sure they've got their badges on straight.'

Well, Jordani, Curly the Preacher, Louis the Greek, the Doc, Butch and me piled into the Boss's car and the place is a pushover. We hardly need to take our gats out of the cases. The hooch is there waiting for us to pick it up like a broad on the sidewalk.

Then some bunch of two-time hoods gate-crash the party muttering something to the effect that the prohibition era's over and try to muscle in on our territory. I mean, you don't do that, baby. It's not nice in a quaint old burgh like Oxford.

The Boss strikes a match and it's rooty-toot-toot for the lot of them. A pity. An honest bootlegger doesn't care to see his liquor adulterated with tomato juice. But like I said…

Oxford Mail 13 December 1968

Michael Bogdanov turned Moliere's comedy, Le Bourgeois Gentilhomme, into a musical he christened The Bootleg

Gentleman for the *Playhouse Company* Christmas show, updating the play to 1930s Chicago and turning the French merchant trying to become an aristocrat into a big-time gangster with social pretensions above his station.

To publicise it I arranged for the cast led by Bill Wallis to visit the brewery for a photoshoot, where my future wife, Sue, took a series of atmospheric pictures of them posing gangster fashion among the giant barrels.

Back at *Mail* features, a cramped office next to the reporters' room with desks for the assistant editor, the features editor, his assistant, Jim McClure, me and my assistant columnist-cum-feature-writer, Doug Boyd, I needed words to match. Jim and Doug, who were fans of crime fiction, supplied them and I wove them into a fanciful story. It proved a lot more eye-catching than the production!

James McClure would go on in 1971 to win the Crime Writers Association Gold Dagger for his first novel, *The Steam Pig*, going one better than the chief subeditor of the *Oxford Times*, Anthony Price, who won the Silver Dagger for his first novel, *The Labyrinth Makers*, in 1970. Tony went on to win the Gold Dagger for *Other Paths to Glory* in 1974. Jim, who succeeded him, first as chief subeditor, then editor of the *Oxford Times*, won the Silver Dagger for *Rogue Eagle* in 1976.

Though highly regarded, neither could match the reputation of the science fiction author, Brian Aldiss, who was the *Oxford Mail* literary editor from 1958 to 1969.

The move to Osney Mead

The 1960s and seventies were a boom time for the Oxford Mail and Times group, as they were for Oxfordshire. The growing affluence of the county brought with it more advertising, an expansion in the number of pages and special supplements. It also created problems. The rise in the number of car owners and the increasing congestion in the city centre meant a former furniture warehouse in New Inn Hall Street was no longer a viable headquarters for a thriving newspaper concern.

The directors toyed with a number of sites. They even considered moving to the building in Botley Road that had started life as the Majestic Cinema, had most recently been Frank Cooper's Oxford Marmalade factory and is now a Waitrose supermarket. In the end they opted for an open plan warehouse in Osney Mead a mile west of the city centre.

BW, who had a passion for architecture, insisted it must be built to the highest standard, which it proved in 1976 by winning a design award. Of greater significance was the press hall with its half-million-pound colour press, the computerised typesetting, the large advertising department with its army of telesales girls, the tea and coffee vending machines, the canteen serving snacks and hot meals, the big carpark one side of the building and the large despatch department the other for the circulation department and delivery van drivers.

In the run-up to the move BW worried that it might take time for our readers to register the change of address and asked if Anthony Wood could do his bit to spell out the transition. I hit on three wheezes.

The first was to ask if any readers had bought furniture from the warehouse in New Inn Hall Street before it became our first home. To my surprise a handful not only still had pieces of furniture bought there, one or two had kept the bills showing how much they paid. Even better my former colleague, the Oxford Mail ex-deputy sports editor, Reg Smith, whose father was foreman there, could give me the entire history of the enterprise. And the icing on the cake: the daughter of the last owner confirmed to me a month later her father sold up rather than get involved in hire purchase.

My second wheeze was to offer an Osney Mead Challenge Trophy for the Oxford and South Midland Amateur Winemakers Festival competitor who produced the best mead. I commissioned a young Yorkshireman who had been a fellow at the Oxford Polytechnic, now Oxford Brookes University, to design it for me and he hit on the idea of a flagon of honey bees floating in resin.

There was no problem finding dead bees. A wet spring and summer had decimated the population. Getting the resin into a flagon without the glass cracking was another matter. After two failed attempts we compromised with a replica of the sort of honeycomb sold in upmarket delicatessens.

It was encased in Perspex and awarded for the first time in October 1973. The winning brew was unbelievably sweet. A threequarters-full bottle remained in my work cupboard looking more and more like a urine sample!

My third wheeze was to make my own journey to our new headquarters by punt. After the last Sports Mail rolled off the presses in New Inn Hall Street on Saturday 19 February 1972 staff set about the logistical exercise that would have us up and running in our new home on Monday.

'Well, here I am at our vast new emporium at Osney Mead,' I began my column, 'but nobody's going to believe the trouble I had getting here. "Look," the editor said to me last St. Christopher's Day, "you know we'll be moving shortly. What are you going to do about your desk? You can't expect Pickford's to cope with that rubbish heap, not to mention your rubber plant, your pumpkins and your barrel of homemade banana chutney."

"That's all right," I said cheerfully, "you tell me how to get there. I've got friends in this town. Old friends. I'll make it." "Very well," he replied dubiously. "Under the Station Bridge. Along the Botley Road as far as St. Frideswide's Church. Turn left at the chip shop [now curry house]." Or words to that effect.'

The jokes would not have been lost on readers of the Anthony Wood Column. St. Christopher was the patron saint of travellers. A recent saga had been about outsize rubber plants and when I went through the mound of papers on my untidy desk, I unearthed a brooch made from the wire of a World War One German zeppelin shot down while trying to bomb London and an unopened jar of banana chutney a reader had made for me.

But I really did intend to travel to Osney Mead by

Unpacking the cracked Osney Mead trophy

punt. I had discovered a backwater of the Thames flowed past the bottom of our car-park and bribed the chap whose father ran the Folly Bridge punt station with a bottle of brandy to take me, loaded a couple of cardboard boxes and a dustbin allegedly containing my possessions aboard and took my seat on a stool, a half-collapsed umbrella protecting me from the weather.

The Thames was in spate. 'Despite Paul's herculean efforts in the engine room, as soon as we got into the main stream we started to drift backwards... "Enough, enough," I cried, "hard to starboard, hard to port. Pass the brandy bottle. For God's sake get me out of here... I'm drowning," then after regaining the shore and my composure I shook him warmly by the hand and hitched a lift from a passing coal lorry.'

It was all fanciful fun. But this classic picture survives of us mid-stream, Paul Hubbocks manfully wielding a paddle, me hunched on my stool. Athar Chaudhry laughed so much taking it from the bank he nearly fell in the river.

Attempting to move to our new offices (photograph Athar Chaudry)

Quotes from the Anthony Wood Column *Oxford Mail*
21 February 1972

10 – John Owen and me

*The doyen of the Reporters' Room at Newspaper House
was John Owen. He had served as an Army captain in
the Second World War and as a result walked with a limp
that some days made it difficult for him to climb the
stairs to the first floor reporters' room. The Army wanted
to amputate his bad leg.*

*Legend had it that at his medical tribunal he refused,
saluted and as he turned to leave fell over. The officer who
helped him up asked: 'Now will you have your leg off,
Captain Owen?' – 'No, I will not!' probably spicing his
reply with a choice expletive.*

*He did the daily police calls and was on first name
terms with everybody from the chief constable down. The
same applied to the university. He knew all the college
heads and bursars, though it was the college porters he
hobnobbed with who gave him most stories. He also
knew quite a few leading politicians as a result of covering the weekly debates at the Oxford Union Society.*

*He drank like a fish. His dog Barnabas went ahead of
him, stopping at ever pub until it was sure he was not
going in. I met him at the Kings Arms on the corner of*

Parks Road and Holywell Street when we covered the university parliament, Congregation, in the Sheldonian Theatre, turning up later and later so I could limit my intake of his favourite tipple, Scotch ale.

He wrote magisterial features on topics like Oxford Treasures and was a talented sketch writer as I learned when I covered the installation of Harold Macmillan as University Chancellor with him. It was a master class in how to convey the atmosphere, pomp and ceremony of an occasion where superficially not much happened.

He took the names at all the major funerals. It was a huge shock to all who wanted to pay their respects when they learnt that he had left instructions his own funeral should be private.

He was fond of me and the column for which he provided tip-offs for many stories and liked my future wife too, particularly after on one of her roving commissions she took a picture of one of his favourite Kings Arms drinking chums sunning himself on a bench in the University Parks, a robin perched alongside him.

Among the celebrities upon whom he liked to call was Sir Basil Blackwell, the legendary head of the world-famous bookshop and publishers, which led to John and me being involved in one of Sir Basil's more unusual enterprises.

His office in Broad Street looked out on the Clarendon Building, the first home of Oxford University Press. The roof was surmounted by lead statues of the nine muses which Sir James Thornhill produced in 1717. Sadly by 1974 Euterpe, the Muse of Music, and Melpomene, the

John Owen and me masquerading as Thomas Hearne and
Anthony à Wood (photograph Bill Radford)

Muse of Tragedy, had toppled from their perches.
    Sir Basil with the University's approval commissioned fibre glass replicas from Richard Kindersley to replace them and funded the lavish ceremony in the Sheldonian Theatre that marked their return. It took the form of one

of those ribald university functions of the eighteenth century at which Terrae Filius, according to the Oxford diarist, Thomas Hearne, 'exposed vice and immorality, and discovered the flagrant crimes of many loose Academicians, particularly the abominable acts of some Heads of Houses'.

The deputy keeper of the Bodleian Library, Hearne was a graduate of St. Edmund Hall. Appropriately another Teddy Hall man, the English don the Revd Graham Midgley, played Terrae Filius on this occasion. My old classics tutor, J.G. Griffith, appeared in a mini-toga in a travesty of his usual role as University Orator and John went as Thomas Hearne, I as my namesake, Anthony à Wood, protesting in his customary cantankerous fashion at being dragged from the seventeenth century to grace a twentieth century occasion. My friends, Betty and Sheila Robbins, who ran the Playhouse Company wardrobe, supplied our wigs and costumes.

11 – A busy life

A featured role in a university production was an indication of how successful the column had become. As George Smith, a friend in the village who would become a Fellow of the Royal Society, put it, it had become the turn to feature in the Oxford Mail. BW recognised the fact by presenting me with the Word's Classics edition of The Life and Times of Anthony à Wood to mark the first anniversary, Charles Fenby's The Other Oxford to mark the tenth.

I had bought Millstone Cottage in Eynsham before Sue and I married but because of major reconstruction it was 1970 before we moved in and those evenings when I was not reviewing, I usually spent decorating or furnishing it with wardrobes and chests of drawers I picked up in secondhand stores and fashioned into built-in units.

Once Katie was born in June 1970, to be followed by Anna in 1972, I became a proud father, first converting rooms into bedrooms for them, then as soon as they were old enough becoming childminder at the weekends to enable Sue to return to work as photographer on a freelance basis, having constructed a darkroom for her where

she could develop and print her films. I also turned my
attention to the garden, laying out fruit and vegetable
patches.

Eynsham is a friendly village and the locals soon came
knocking as I recalled in an article for the Witney
Gazette after I retired.

Leave well alone

The chap renovating the terraced cottage next door has
found a well in his back garden. Sue and I wonder if it
might be ours. No, we don't think he's pinched it, nor that
it has hopped over the wall like the cat. But we have lost a
well… or rather never found it.

After we moved into Millstone Cottage in 1970 a surprising number of older villagers stopped us in the street to
inform us that they'd lived where we did in their youth.
Surprising, that is, until you take account of the fact that
our large four-bedroomed home had once been three
small, one-up, one-down, terraced cottages.

We would invite them in, laugh at their stories, especially the one about the night the iron bedstead leg came
through the living room ceiling. Don't ask me how that
happened! We'd tell them about the brass-knobbed bedstead the workmen had found in the attic above our garage
and our disappointment when they had to saw it in half to
get it through the trapdoor. We'd show them the silver
fourpenny piece I'd found under one of the bedroom
window sills.

Then we'd take them into the back garden and sooner or later they'd all ask the same question: 'Have you still got the well?' 'No,' we'd say. 'Where was it?' A look of bewilderment would cloud their faces. 'Over there,' they'd say, pointing vaguely. But they weren't sure. 'It was such a long time ago…' In the end I got Eynsham's general stores proprietor, Bill Sawyer, who reckoned to be a bit of a water diviner, to come with his withy sticks. I dug where they twitched. I dug and I dug. Eventually I had enough gravel to lay our patio, but I never did find the well. I filled the hole in again, ruefully recalling the story Bud Flanagan used to tell Chesney Allen when they were a top music hall double act in the 1930s.

Bud maintained he'd once earned his living digging holes and selling them to farmers in Africa… 'I dug a hole for a farmer and he wouldn't have it,' he recalled. Ches: 'Why not?' Bud: 'It was two feet too short. Well, I wasn't going to waste a good hole like that… I pulled it out the ground and when I'd got it out the farmer wanted it. The trouble was I couldn't get it back.' Ches: 'You couldn't get the hole back?' Bud: 'No – I'd bent it!'

But my favourite story concerns St. Margaret's Well at Binsey. That's the so-called treacle or healing well by the Thames in West Oxford sick pilgrims used to flock to in medieval times in hopes of a cure. It's also the origin of that fictitious source of sweetness, Binsey Treacle Mine.

By the second half of the nineteenth century the well was in a sad state of repair and a Christ Church don called Prout, who at the time was the incumbent at Binsey Church, decided to restore it at his own expense. When the job reached completion, he thought it would be a nice idea to record his generosity with a stone tablet and invited his fellow dons to suggest a suitable inscription.

The scholars strove to outdo one another with their learning. The Revd Charles Lutwidge Dodgson remained silent. 'Well?' asked Prout. The shy mathematics don, better known as Lewis Carroll, the creator of *Alice in Wonderland*, smiled sweetly. 'Leave well alone?' he suggested.

Witney Gazette 4 May 1995

Both Sue and I became heavily involved in village life. She helped launch the Acre End Playgroup and village ballet school, became a leading member of the Eynsham Society, later a primary school governor and finally an assistant in the village library. I by a succession of flukes found myself founding the Eynsham and District branch of West Oxfordshire Liberal Association, chairing the village's Queen's Silver Jubilee Committee, becoming chair of the village youth club and a comprehensive school governor.

Why I am a Liberal

1933 was a bad year for the Liberal Party, a strange beast with three crumpled horns all pointing in different directions. Yet I believe I was born a Liberal. I cannot remember a time when I entertained any other political philosophy, even in the volatile atmosphere of mock elections at school.

At fourteen a friend tried to interest me in the Young

Conservatives and at twenty-three I actually belonged to them for a few months. But in Keighley that had no more political significance than belonging to the Liberal Club. One was the only meeting place for young people apart from the Saturday night hop at the Mechanics Institute. The other was the only place you could rely on getting a late-night drink after eleven o'clock.

There were active Liberals in the Yorkshire West Riding mill town. Some six or seven grey haired stalwarts met to discuss aspects of Liberal policy from time to time with dispassionate honesty, and since word seemed not to have filtered through to the *Keighley News* that the Westminster Press had long since abandoned its Liberal pretensions it was my job to chronicle their deliberations.

Whether readers appreciated my thousand word dissertations on topics like *Possible Effects of Co-Ownership on the Co-op* I do not know, but it was the only political education I had and these old-fashioned seminars, the like of which I have not encountered since, must have helped my thinking a great deal.

Back in Oxford three years later in 1959 I covered my first General Election for the *Oxford Mail* and in 1964 followed the fortunes of the successful Conservative candidate, Monty Woodhouse, for the same paper. I festooned the wall behind my desk with Tory slogans and blue-ribboned graphs much to the irritation of my Socialist colleague who followed the fortunes of the Labour candidate.

Then on the eve of the poll, after covering my last assignment of the campaign, I tore them all down and replaced them with the favours of that much more rumbustious

Liberal candidate, Ivor Davies.

Monty presented me with an autographed copy of one of his books in gratitude for my faithful reporting of his fight and I should have presented his agent with a bust of Lloyd George in gratitude for what he taught me about political organisation.

Back then I still believed journalistic detachment stopped short of party membership and it was to be another ten years before I changed my mind. In the run-up to the February 1974 General Election as a result of the orange poster in our window the ardent campaigner, Mary Thomson, twisted my wife's arm and a tea-party took place at our house to meet Robert Sparrow, Mid-Oxfordshire's first Liberal candidate since 1910.

Nearly fifty people from all over Eynsham crowded into our living room and it was obvious somebody had to mobilise them. I took the plunge. From an ironic observer of life who believed the Liberal view must ultimately prevail I changed overnight to an active campaigner for the renaissance of the Liberal movement.

Mid-Oxon Liberal Association Newsletter October-November 1976 Volume 1 Number 12

Between delving into local history and reflecting other readers' passions Anthony Wood continued to provide a fund of amusing stories and some pretty macabre ones too. What follows has taken on an even more gruesome significance in the light of two trials for child murder in 2021 and another looming in 2022.

Sweet Fanny Adams

My story concerns Sweet Fanny Adams and if you think that means I've got nothing better to write about today, you're wrong. In our day Fanny Adams may be a polite way of saying something's of no consequence, but in the nineteenth century she really existed and her sad end spawned a number of expressions from Victorian sailors using her name to describe their unsavoury meat rations* to twentieth century Australian World War One soldiers employing it as a euphemism for a considerably more vulgar term**.

I am indebted for the tale to Eric Johnson, who used to work in the Oxford University Land Agent's Department. Back in 1969 I wrote an article about his interest in folk songs and another about his quest for *The Ballad of the Wytham Miller*. Since then, he'd taken a course at a London teacher training college and at the age of fifty embarked on a new career as Lecturer in Liberal Studies at Southampton Technical College. It was soon after his arrival there that a colleague introduced him to Sweet Fanny Adams.

The daughter of a bricklayer at Alton in Hampshire, she was just eight years and four months old on 24 August 1867 when she fell foul of Frederick Baker, a clerk in a local solicitor's office, but let the *Oxford Times* take up the story.

'A crime was committed at Alton on Saturday after-

* First recorded by Barrière and Leland in A Dictionary of Slang, Jargon and Cant in 1889.
** First recorded by Walter Downing, an Australian First World War soldier, as Sweet Fanny Adams, or rather her initials, being a euphemism for 'sweet fuck all' in Diggers Dialects in 1919.

noon,' it reported in its issue of Saturday 31 August 1867, 'which for brutality throws all recent murders into the shade. A band of children were in a meadow near Alton Church when a young man passing by distributed some coppers among the group. He then spoke to a pretty little girl about eight years of age named Adams.

'According to the story of the other children he endeavoured to get her to accompany him into a hop plantation close at hand. She was evidently reluctant to go and the man carried her off in his arms. Later in the day, the little girl was missed by her parents, and a search was made.

'The first indication of foul play was the discovery of a pool of blood near the entrance to the plantation. A little further on the searchers came upon the dissevered head of the poor child, which rested on a hop pole, then on a portion of the trunk cut open and the heart couped out, and then on one arm, leaving the lower part of the trunk and the other arm undiscovered.

'On Sunday morning the missing arm was found and clenched in the hand was a halfpenny. From the information gleaned from the children who were at play with the deceased a young man employed in a solicitor's office in this town was apprehended on Saturday evening on suspicion.'

The *Oxford Times* said Frederick Baker, who came of well-to-do parents, was a slim man standing about five feet four inches high, weighing some eight stone. He was described as being of reserved demeanour and very old-fashioned and methodical in his habits. Certainly, both before and after his arrest he showed a finical attention to financial detail.

When Fanny's playmate, Minnie Warner cried: 'That's the man who gave us the pennies,' he immediately corrected her: 'No, it was three halfpennies I gave you and the others a halfpenny,' and he also put right the police superintendent who added up the contents of his pockets wrongly.

At the police station he maintained his innocence for a long time. 'When the blood on his wristbands was pointed out to him the prisoner rubbed his hands together and intently observed them for a short time, when he replied: "Well, I don't see a cut or scratch on my hand to account for the blood." The fact of the prisoner having one of his trouser legs wet being represented to him, Baker answered: "Well, that won't hang me, will it?"'

He displayed the same remarkable callousness in his attitude to the crime. At the inquest on Fanny a fellow clerk, Maurice Biddle, described how Baker had arranged to leave Alton with the 'boots' of the Swan Tap the Monday after the murder.

'I can turn my hand to anything,' scoffed the young man employed by the inn to polish the customers' footwear in the days when ways were foul in winter, deep in dust in summer, 'but you can't!' To which Baker retorted: 'Yes, I could turn butcher.' What incensed the public more than anything was the entry the police found in Baker's diary for August 24: 'Killed a young girl. It was fine and hot.'

After the jury had returned a verdict of wilful murder an angry mob collected outside the hostelry where the inquest was held and as he waited with his custodians to make the

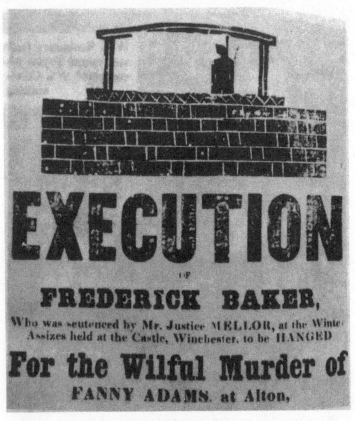

Fanny Adams broadsheet

dash to the local lock-up the enormity of his deed must at last have begun to dawn on him. He was duly found guilty at Hampshire Winter Assizes in Winchester Castle and was sentenced by Mr Justice Mellor to be hanged.

The execution took place on Christmas Eve. 'The behaviour of the vast crowd,' the *Oxford Times* reported, 'was most exemplary and on the culprit appearing on the scaffold he was received with solemn silence. It is satisfying to add that Baker had made a full and complete confession of the crime, which he attributes to an indulgence in strong drink.' He was 'launched into eternity' and receded into obscurity.

His unfortunate victim remained in common parlance, not as it happens because of the gruesomeness of her death, but because at the time the Admiralty was engaged in a search for a more satisfactory diet than salted meat for the scurvy-ridden crews of the men o' wars. The solution adopted by the Royal Navy was to chop mutton up in little pieces and can it, and it wasn't long before some nautical wag christened it Sweet Fanny Adams.

Eric Johnson's fascination for the story came from the fact that it prompted two ballads. 'I know they're morbid,' he said, 'but I think they're interesting as a reminder of the way in which songs and ballads would be made up about murders and executions as well as a great many other things, and they give us an insight into aspects of our history academic writers overlook.'

Anthony Wood Column *Oxford Mail* 28 December 1972

Your first motor car sir? Allow me...

Another interview with a reader prompted him to lend me a copy of the motoring catalogue Gamages of Holborn, a leading London department store from 1878 to 1972, issued – surprisingly – in the middle of the First World War.

Now sir, as to colour, the Calcott Light Car comes in standard grey, but it is a simple matter to paint it any colour you or madam may desire. Just £1 extra, and there are a number of other extras I should like to draw your attention to. A dickey seat, so useful for taking serving maids on picnics, thrilling mothers-in-law and accommodating younger members of the family – that is £4 10s.

Then a dynamo lighting set will bring the price of your new motorcar to £210, an extra £15, and a dynamo lighting set and electric self-starter will bring the price to £225. Madam is afraid of electricity and sir thinks batteries or accumulators might be rather messy? Well, it is a point of view, perhaps carbide, acetylene, gas, petroleum or paraffin?

You will find a comprehensive selection of the most up-to-date methods of illumination in *Gamages 1915 Motorists Catalogue*. You'll stick to the horse and carriage after dark. Very good, sir. But you think a warning instrument...

I'm glad you mentioned that. The newest device on the market is the exhaust pipe horn or whistle. Then there are various horns with rubber bulbs. The Boa Constrictor horn is rather fun. Something of which I am fond is the motor foot gong, a bit loud, sir, but very musical. Or there is the Gamage mouth siren, better for clearing sleepy carters out of the way than even the loud mechanical sirens.

I don't suppose I can interest you in tools, oils or car cleaning sundries? No. Well, if you leave the groom to attend to that side of things, sir, perhaps you would be so kind as to consider investing in a motor cleaning outfit for him. We had a case recently of an ostler trying to curry-comb the roof canopy of a distinguished customer's Model T Ford.

We can supply a set of best quality brushes and polishing materials in a box for twenty-five shillings, and something some customers find exceedingly useful is the new and ingenious water brush attached to a hose which brushes and washes the wheels and body of the car.

A mascot? The lucky Lincoln Imp has become known to fame as a potent charm against danger and police traps. The Robert Mascot has a moveable head, which allows some very funny expressions. Then there are The Goddess of Speed, The Flying Fox, a Bulldog, a Lion Rampant or, ah yes, the Flags of the Nations, so patriotic and becoming in these troubled times.

Now, clothing. As this is your first motor-car I think I should offer a word of advice about protecting yourselves from the weather. You will have seen from your trial spins that the greater velocity of the automobile subjects its occupants to a greater buffeting from the elements.

For you, sir, I would respectfully recommend combination goggles to prevent dust and rain getting into your eyes and ear guards to protect your ears from cold and wet, and to obviate buzzing noises which can be so irritating on fast cars.

For you, madam, a foot muff or in winter weather an everlasting foot-warmer. Since you live in North Oxford-shire, sir, you might also care to consider a steering-wheel muff, which ensures warmth and comfort for the hands and wrists without interfering with the steering.

In the summer I am sure madam would look very becoming in a Holland, crush or tussore silk dustcoat, while sir might favour the Epsom rainproof dustcoat or the Goodwood rainproof gabardine dustcoat.

Madam is right. The summer months are the best for motoring. If you fancy a day's outing into the countryside, Gamages can offer several attractive tea and luncheon cases complete with all fittings. There is an adjustable motor sunshade to keep the sun and wind off madam's face and sundry other useful inventions.

A breakdown, sir? That is something we try not to think about, but if sir and madam would care to step this way, we will try to put your minds at rest by showing you some of the wonderful devices the architects of the new age – I hope you will not think me over-romantic – have designed to overcome the little difficulties the motorist may meet along the way.

Take the tyre puttee, a device, sir, a military gentleman like yourself will appreciate. Should you be so unlucky as to run over a bottle and damage your tyre, you buckle the puttee securely to a spoke, roll it round the affected spot, fasten the other end to another convenient spoke, inflate your tyre and away you go.

Means of inflation? How silly of me. You should find a foot-pump in your tool kit, but what about the Gamage pure air engine pump, which saves your time, tyres, temper and physical strength. Just remove a spark plug and... Spark plugs, madam? Here, let me show you what they are.

How do you remove them, sir? Pardon me, while I slip on a sleeve protector and find a box spanner. Right, a

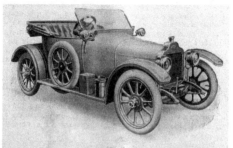

Calcott light car complete with standard body and equipment.

The Calcott Light Car (above); Brooklands coat to keep sir warm and for madam the Motura coat with detachable leather lining (Gamages' 1915 Motoring Catalogue)

simple turn. Uggh! A simple turn. Ugggghh! A simple turn. Uugggggghhh! Damn these blacksmiths turned mechanics.

No, madam, I assure you I am not losing my temper. It's just a matter of time, sir, I assure you. Believe me, I will move it. I swear to you as I am a Methodist, I was not so blasphemous as to say the Lord give me strength!

Anthony Wood Column *Oxford Mail* 19 August 1977

Reading my handwriting

Canon Tom South of Deddington has never met me, yet he asserts with confidence – and I would be the last to disagree! – that I am intelligent, capable and friendly. Nice to be told that, isn't it? True, the learned canon reckons these qualities are sometimes hidden behind a slightly austere front, that at times I lack drive, and that I tend to be rather set in my ways, but these mild criticisms are included in what is otherwise such a delightful encomium that I feel bound to accept them.

Just listen to some of the other pleasant things the canon has to say about me: I am honest, frank, prudently generous, well-organised, kind, considerate to others, loyal to standards and traditions, dignified and self-confident. I ought to be blushing as I enumerate them but – you may have already guessed it – modesty is not a quality Canon South discerns.

How is it that the canon knows so much about me? It's my handwriting that gives me away. And is the portrait Canon South paints after lengthy graphological analysis of a sample of my handwriting accurate? Well, to be serious,

I am hardly qualified to say, but my colleagues all agree that it's astonishingly exact.

Only one claim surprises them – that I am tidy-minded. But then again, they have seen (and Canon South has not) my desk piled high with papers, books and used coffee cups. Yet at least I know where to lay my hands on any document I want so I suppose that is tidy-mindedness of sorts.

As I said, Canon South has not met me. His character assessment was based solely on less than 200 words of my writing – an extract from the short biography of my namesake Anthony à Wood in the *Encyclopaedia Britannica* – and the knowledge that I am male, fortyish and presumably right-handed. One advantage of a penname, you see, is that Canon South had no idea I was Anthony Wood.

I dispatched my assistant to interview him at his home, Folly Cottage, Deddington, with the writing sample and firm instructions that he was to keep his mouth shut about my identity. For once he obeyed me.

Canon South took up graphology when he retired in 1972 as Rector of Latimer, near Chesham, and returned 'home' to Deddington. He had married and served his first curacy in Banbury and had been Vicar of Adderbury from 1939–47. 'I was looking for some parttime occupation, partly as a mental stimulant and partly to earn a little pocket money to supplement my pension. Then I saw an advertisement in a newspaper for a correspondence course in graphology and thought that seemed just the thing.

'I have always been interested in handwriting. My first job was a bank clerk and I used to find myself looking with great interest at the signatures on the various forms. Some pieces of handwriting I could remember years later. I made superficial judgments about people, but of course I wasn't qualified then.'

Which prompts the question: now he is trained does he find himself making more precise judgments on the basis of handwriting he receives, and do his friends hesitate for fear of being analysed to send any but typewritten letters? 'No, of course not. For one thing I haven't the time. Each study involves up to fifty tests and takes about five hours.'

Canon South does not pretend that graphology is an exact science: its success rate is about eighty-five per cent – accurate enough to give him no qualms of conscience when he gives a confidential analysis for employers on the characters of would-be workers, or when he offers to provide guidance on a couple's likely compatibility for marriage (a pity he wasn't qualified when he officiated at countless weddings as a full-time cleric!)

'While not exact, graphology nevertheless has a scientific basis of a psychological character related to the fact that handwriting, once mature, is very largely a conditional reflex. A few loops and flourishes may be consciously drawn, but the formation of most letters and lines, the placing and shaping of i-dots and t-bars, the pressure, spacing and margins – and there are many more features – tend to be executed without conscious thought and thus reflect the character of the writer.'

To give a couple of examples of the technique used to analyse my sample (it would be impossible to summarise the canon's four-page report): 'The general openness of style, with its lack of elaboration, is a sign of honesty and frankness, while the plain drawing of many letters – "Wood" on line three, "of" on line nine – suggests that the writer likes to get to the point without wasting time on nonessentials.'

'A degree of caution in money matters is likely to be combined with prudent generosity (the open "a"s and "o") – material rewards probably matter very little compared to job satisfaction (the lean and small development of the "I" and the "x").' And so it continues. But I think you can see the idea.

Canon South's conclusion – actually it was at the beginning of the report – is that the picture is rather like that of the traditional Scotsman*. Well, I don't think anyone's said that to me before!

Anthony Wood Column *Oxford Mail* 19 November 1975

Indian summer of the flea

What I liked about flea circuses when I was a boy was the moment when the ringmaster rolled up his shirtsleeve. 'I expect you have been wondering, ladies and gentlemen,' he would say conspiratorially, 'how I keep the stars of my show in such wonderful condition. Well, it involves great

---

* It was certainly in my blood. My great-grandmother on my father's side was a Scot from Rothes at the head of the Spey Valley. She married my great-grandfather, a Cockney from Stepney, while working as a governess at Bangalore in India, where he was serving as a gunner in the Royal Horse Artillery.

personal sacrifice.' Then, as the crowd watched in fascin-ated horror, he would pick up one of his miniscule per-formers, deposit it on his forearm and invite the insect to take its fill.

It was a splendid piece of showmanship, but I realise now it was all a con. He didn't allow the fleas to suck his blood. After the fair was over, he took them back to his caravan and let them plug into the cat.

Cat fleas, as a lot of us in Oxfordshire have been finding out recently, are amazingly tough, resilient creatures, quite capable of pulling miniature chariots, dragging matchstick logs across cotton tightropes, and all the other stunts that used to keep us agog. But while they will in emergency take a snack from the odd, carefully chosen human being like my wife, it is upon feline blood they depend for their health and prosperity.

In the old days there were crude but effective ways of dealing with them. My father remembers discovering our cat was infested on one occasion when my mother was in hospital. He took the unfortunate moggie into the garden and dowsed it liberally with Keating's Powder. The fleas flew off in one direction, the cat flew off in the other and, though it didn't return home for a week, when it did it was clean.

Now such quick-acting repellents have disappeared from the market, presumably because of the limitations on the use of DDT. There is an aerosol available, which we think would keep the fellow travellers who keep infiltrating our ginger tom, Fred, in check, but we have only to go to the cupboard where it is kept and Fred is off. He simply can't stand a can which emits a hiss like a snake.

We have to make do with inferior proprietary powders, which he tolerates in small doses, a flea collar with bell that scares more birds than fleas, and a flea comb, which he enjoys when he is in the mood. The idea is that the gap between the teeth is so narrow that once trapped there the fleas can't escape until you slide them off into a cup of diluted washing up liquid and instant death. But it is a painfully laborious process and, as the vet pointed out to my wife, you miss three fleas for every one you catch.

Not that he needed to tell Sue that. She keeps pieces of moistened soap all over the house on which she can trap the fleas that hop onto her before they have a chance to hop off again. We have autumn-cleaned all the rooms, aired the carpets, washed the curtains, and go around spraying every nook or cranny where the unwelcome squatters might be lurking or have laid their eggs. Yet still they persist, in the kitchen, in the bathroom, even in bed.

Am I the only husband returning late from the office who must switch on the light in order to convince his wife he's not climbing in with somebody else?

The fleas don't attack me, nor do they bite our two daughters as voraciously as my wife, though Katie is more susceptible than Anna. Nonetheless, I find myself itching and scratching in sympathy and stalking every stray biscuit crumb in case it should jump.

The only consolation I have is that I don't have to conceal my irritation. I can broadcast it to the world. There is no social stigma any more about having fleas. My mother recalls a visit by my grandmother many years ago. 'Violet,'

Fleas (Jim Needle cartoon)

she announced when she came downstairs after unpacking, 'I found a flea in my bed.' 'Well, there are no fleas in my house, mum,' bridled my mother. 'You must have brought it with you.'

Eventually my grandmother salved her conscience and my mother's pride by declaring that my father had brought the offending creature back from the stable in Headington Quarry where he kept his pony. But as the owner indignantly affirmed, he hadn't.

'Oh, Mrs Chapman,' confessed a neighbour when my mother told her the story after my grandmother had returned to London, 'I would never have dared to tell you. I'm so ashamed. But we've been absolutely infested with the things.' So it turned out had our neighbour on the other side, and onto what we thought were garden bonfires they had been piling flea-ridden carpets, curtains, pillows and cushions.

Today it is different. 'How are you, Sue?' calls the vicar's

wife cheerily. 'Fine,' says my wife, 'apart from the fleas,' and a crowd of mums collapse in mirth outside Eynsham Primary School gates.

But suppose we aren't experiencing the Indian summer of the cat flea? Suppose the pest control officers of the various district councils aren't able to keep the situation under control? Suppose, if you will pardon the pun, the spring of the cat flea is to come?

This summer we went up to the northwest coast of Scotland as we do most summers to visit my wife's parents and there it wasn't cat fleas that was plaguing them, it was sheep ticks. To the layman sheep ticks have a lot in common with cat fleas. But they are much bigger and much nastier, and they can hang on a lot longer waiting for a suitable victim.

When they have gorged themselves, they drop off to lay their eggs and at that stage they look like miniature haggises with obscene, gesticulating eyebrows, which before they blew themselves up with blood, it gradually dawns on you, were perfectly respectable legs. If they can't find a convenient sheep to feed on, they usually attack dogs, but one night my youngest woke me up in the small hours to inform me one had attached itself to the midriff* of her cousin.

Attached was the word. Most of the tick came away with my tweezers, but the jaws of the creature remained embedded in the skin of my niece. In the circumstances she was surprisingly philosophical about it, just dabbed the angry red spot with a dash of antiseptic liquid and went back to sleep.

But when I read later that the Scottish grouse season had been an almost total disaster – the tick-ridden game birds were so anaemic they couldn't get off the ground – it touched a raw nerve, and the persistent cat fleas have played on it. I see myself with a spent Flit-gun, powerless before the advancing hordes.

'I only caught two today,' Sue tells me. Furious combing of Fred produces only one and that looks suspiciously like a dog flea (we haven't got a dog). A friend suggests we drink to celebrate our famous victory. But I'm not convinced. I tell him: 'You wait a tick…' Then I groan as I realise what I've said. There's no stopping them. They've invaded my subconscious now.

Oxford Mail 14 November 1978

---

* Actually, it was her groin, but I spared her, myself, and my readers that embarrassment!

12 – Moving down market

BW tried to maintain the standards HT had set, to ensure the Oxford Mail continued to be a paper the rest of the world looked up to. But its continuing expansion and prosperity meant a broadening in scope and a much wider range of features. One I was responsible for came about by accident. A leading firm that specialised in restaurant guides decided to branch out into travel guides and commissioned me to compile the section on Oxford, detailing all the different aspects they wanted me to cover.

I warned them the material would be enough to fill a book, but they persisted so I sent them some sixty closely typed pages, then heard nothing more from them. Finally, months later they admitted they had dropped the project and reluctantly paid me for my labours. Not wanting to waste my efforts, I suggested it could form the basis of what proved to be one of our biggest money spinners, an annual Oxford Mail Leisure Guide. It was issued free with the paper, then went on sale to tourists.

Pearson plc had owned what became the Westminster Press Group of provincial newspapers since 1921, adding to it its one national newspaper, the Financial Times, in

1957. In the 1970s it began to take a more hands-on approach to the running of them.

In 1979 it moved BW to London and transferred Terry Page from the Brighton Argus, a rakish character with an engaging manner, to replace him. It led to a change of role for me, which after fifteen years as the paper's columnist was probably overdue.

When the Press Association announced that John Paul II was to become the first Pope in history to visit Ireland and papers wishing to cover the event should apply to the Catholic Press Office, keen to make a splash, Terry at once sought permission from Westminster Press to cover it on behalf of the group and asked me to do the job.

On 21 September 1979 a banner headline boasted: 'When the Pope starts his visit to Eire next week the Oxford Mail will be there. Don Chapman, staff special writer, has been accredited to the press team covering the historic tour.'

For a while I continued writing the Anthony Wood Column three days a week but it was no longer the main feature on the leader page. Instead, I contributed a steady stream of offbeat and more serious features under my own name.

Pay as you burn

You can understand the frustration of people when they stuff their electricity meter full of ten-p pieces, then the Southern Electricity Board won't come and collect their hard burnt cash. But the quartet in Divinity Road, Oxford, who wrote to the *Oxford Star* to complain about their 'damned jammed meter' had only themselves to blame according to the Oxford District manager, Alwyn Eato.

'If they're spending that sort of money on electricity,' he said, 'they'd be much better off with a credit meter and a quarterly bill like the majority of householders in the Oxford area.' What sort of money he wouldn't specify because he didn't want to start a spate of meter thefts, but it probably wouldn't take most people long to work out how much four people sharing a rented house can clock up in thirteen weeks.

Given the winter weather in 1979–80, secretary Pippa Griffith, computer scientist John Appleyard, teacher Pauline Taylor and medical student Steve Howell could easily squeeze £80 into their coin box with a bit of banging.

By hitting the meter hard on the side, they claimed in their letter to the *Star*, the SEB at Yarnton had advised them they might be able to persuade it to accept more money. And since there are now five of them trying to keep warm in their separate rooms, they could quite possibly reach £100 if the meter didn't fall off the wall first, as they alleged it was about to do.

Mr Eato didn't encourage meter-bashing. If the inmates did theirs a permanent injury, they could end up paying for a replacement as well as for a collector making a special visit to empty the one they'd battered to death. In the inflationary times Britain was going through the fact was slot meters simply couldn't keep pace with multi-occupational households.

To be honest, Mr Eato said, the electricity boards would have liked to do away with them altogether, but the consumer protection organisations were against the idea. Old people, they pointed out, trying to scrape a living on modest pensions, preferred to pay as they burned, and the SEB accepted they had a point.

The trouble was landlords of rented property also liked slot meters because it removed the possibility of them having to settle the bills of fly-by-night tenants, and tenants made up the bulk of the ten to fifteen per cent of consumers in the Oxford area who paid through the slot for their electricity.

It also meant paying through the nose for their supplies because, Mr Eato said, it would hardly be fair to lumber all consumers with the extra costs involved in meter emptying, and that was why he was constantly showering the public with leaflets pointing out that there were less painful ways to pay than living on bread and water for a fortnight whenever the bills for the winter quarter of the year came in.

But while a friendly social worker might persuade an old age pensioner of the advantage of opening a budget account, it was much harder to convince a landlord. There were no advantages as far as he was concerned unless the thought of demure young misses flailing their tiny frozen hands against the sides of unyielding meters caused him to take pity on them.

In any case it had to be said not all demure young misses favoured the conversion to credit meters. Cheerful Pauline Taylor from New Zealand where they didn't have slot meters for electricity was against the idea before I called. Nine people had lived at forty-one Divinity Road in the past year and as the resident of longest standing she'd got the job of chasing them up to pay their share of a lately arrived £125 telephone bill.

'I suppose it is exceptional to have that high a turnover of residents,' she said, 'and I suppose it is exceptional for a bill to be delayed so long by a strike, but when it happens it does make you think. As a matter of fact, the boys wanted to change to a credit meter before Christmas. One of them had been ill and after jumping in and out of bed to stuff coins in the slot meter it was too much when the SEB refused to come and empty the thing.

'But I said no. I wasn't going to go round the house trying to screw money out of people to pay electricity bills as well as telephone bills and rate bills so he let off steam by writing to the *Star* instead.'

After hearing that Mr Eato thought she was mad she was having second thoughts and when I left was all set to have a powwow with the rest of the inmates, then approach the landlord. If there's any commission on conversions the SEB might think about knocking ten per cent off my next bill!

Oxford Mail 10 January 1980

Coin-in-the-slot electricity – and gas! – prepayment meters have a long history. But by the 1980s increasing thefts led prime minister Margaret Thatcher to launch a campaign for their removal. They finally disappeared

'Pat says not to worry, he's got a key!' (Jim Needle cartoon)

from private homes at the beginning of the twenty-first century, but landlords still use them in various forms including electronic smart meters to make sure their tenants don't default.

The *Oxford Star* was a weekly free sheet the Oxford Mail and Times group produced from 1976 to 2013.

Death then and now

The simplest way to bury a cat is to dig a hole in a corner of the garden and cover it over – but you can't do that to grandma. Death remains an occasion for pomp and circumstance.

The funeral corteges may have to queue up outside the cemetery gates of Britain's larger cities. The mourners may have to thread their way through acres of monumental masonry to reach the graveside of the dear departed, but a lot of us cling grimly to what we fondly and mistakenly regard as the time-honoured ritual of burial: the black limousines, the dark suits and dresses, the uneasy wake, the horrendous slabs of marble.

We are making life more and more difficult for the people who provide the land in which we inter our dead. Despite the growth in popularity of cremation, which now claims two-thirds of our corpses, a sizeable number of people still prefer burial. I do myself. Nothing to do with religion or any nonsense about wanting to lie with my ancestors: as a keen occasional gardener I like to think of myself as a lump of human compost, which will one day return to the soil some of the goodness I have taken out of it, provided of course I don't die of some dreaded disease.

Such an attitude is not common. Since man first became a social animal, he has tended to surround death with an air of mystique. Some primitive societies have stowed away their corpses as if they were embarking on a long journey, others in a posture of sleep. Some have put them out for the birds to peck at, reverentially gathering up the bones in a jar. Some have even tried to preserve their loved ones for posterity by embalming them, just as today some Americans prefer deep-freezing to burial in the hope that one day scientists will be able to defrost them again.

In medieval Britain it was all quite simple. The villagers carried their dead to church in a communal coffin and after the burial service tipped them out into the earth in a winding sheet. If they were a lord or lady their relatives might be able to afford a marble monument. If they were a knight or some other important person they might run to a brass. Otherwise, all they got was a humble wooden cross.

In fifty to one hundred years' time when it and the body underneath had rotted away there was no need for the sexton to stand on ceremony. When he ran out of space in his churchyard, he dug a new hole on top of the old one and any bones he found he put in the church's charnel house or dug in again.

'Alas, poor Yorick, I knew him well, Horatio,' Shakespeare made Hamlet say in the famous tragedy when the gravedigger unearthed the skull of the king's jester, but there was no question of him running the clumsy workman through with his rapier for disturbing the last resting place of a celebrated courtier. It was just the cue for a few well-chosen apostrophes on the subject of mortality.

The same healthy attitude to death persisted until the Industrial Revolution. Then the boom in the population of our towns started posing problems with which the old-fashioned graveyards could no longer cope. Outbreaks of cholera, typhoid and diphtheria paved the way for the

Burial Act of 1853, still the main legislation on interment, and the Victorian love of monuments ensured that cemeteries no longer had a steady turnover. They started to fill up.

In Switzerland there is actually a law encouraging the removal of the remains of former occupants from church-yards so that they can be used again and again, and one or two enlightened authorities in Britain I'm told operate a similar form of rotation in their cemeteries. When one half fills up it lies fallow for fifty or a hundred years while they fill up the other half. Then they remove the bones and monuments from the first half and start all over again.

More often what happens is the poor sexton reaches the stage where he can't squeeze in another grave without disturbing those that are there already. He tells the parson. The parson tells the Diocesan Registrar. The Registrar puts him in touch with the Department of the Environment, and the Department sends a questionnaire.

The parson stands a strong chance of success if he can satisfy the Department there is no room left in the church-yard, to bury more people there would constitute a health hazard, or it is 'contrary to decency'. In other words, the poor parson might enrage me or my family by accidentally exhuming the half-rotted remains of dear Aunt Jemima because we were too mean to mark her grave with a head-stone or upset the Mothers' Union by trying to slot in past-president Mrs Green between Mrs Black and Mrs White, with whom she never got on.

The Department then contacts the parish and district councils concerned. They quietly do their nuts because they will have to provide a new burial ground unless the church is far-sighted or lucky enough to have earmarked land for an extension and, provided no one during this lengthy process of consultation comes up with a valid reason why the churchyard should remain open, the Department reluctantly applies to the Privy Council for an Order in Council approving its closure.

This complicated procedure is necessary because under Common Law a person has the right to lie with his ancestors in a parish churchyard. As part of the Establishment, the Church of England has to accept more or less anybody who comes. The reluctance stems from the fact that not only does the Department dislike lumbering local authorities with the problems and expense of providing new burial grounds.

Under the 1972 Local Government Act, which is what you might call the enabling legislation, once a graveyard is closed a parson can ask a local authority to take over responsibility for its upkeep and maintenance. Nevertheless, the Privy Council continues to grant Orders in Council at an alarming rate. The latest in the Oxford area in 1980 was at North Hinksey, fortunately little more than a stone's throw away from Botley Cemetery, and parsons and local authorities continue to give warnings that their churchyards and cemeteries are filling up.

My own village of Eynsham was in the process of acquiring another burial ground to replace its centuries-old churchyard which would be 'full' in a couple of years' time and Banbury would need another twenty acre site in 1984.

Closure doesn't quite mean what it says. The Vicar of

North Hinksey, the Revd John Crisp, pointed out: 'Providing the last interment was below three feet we are allowed to add members of the family, so it is quite usual for us to have interments. But in nearly every case the coffin comes from a long way away because the member of the family has moved.'

He had some sympathy with the idea of using churchyards over and over again as his predecessors must have done in times past. But whereas modern mass-produced gravestones tend to look hideous, he said the old ones were nearly always beautiful and a well-maintained country churchyard with ancient gravestones could look a delight 'as indeed the old part of North Hinksey churchyard did and does'.

Despite that argument and most people's regard for these forms of ancient monument, it is obvious we can't go on indefinitely scratching around for new burial grounds. Otherwise, we shall end up with vast disused cemeteries that are little better than junkyards of monumental masonry. Shortage of arable land will demand mass incineration, and how long then I wonder before the crematoria start running out of places to plant all those memorial tablets, rose trees and urns?

I can quite understand the feelings of people who rather fancy the idea of departing this life as a handful of ashes. Scattered over the green on the golf course where you once nearly scored a hole in one. Quietly slipped in a brown paper bag into the foundations of the vast new supermarket where you once ran a homely corner shop. You have to admit it is a satisfying end.

Resting in peace under the runner beans (Jim Needle cartoon)

But frankly it doesn't appeal to me. So long as my existence is recorded for posterity in a register somewhere in the bowels of Somerset House, so long as some computer doesn't hiccup and despatch those brief records into oblivion, I am not even bothered about having a little wooden cross. I am quite content like William Wordsworth's Lucy to be 'rolled around in earth's diurnal course with rocks and stones and trees' in the hope that when Nature has completed recycling me, I may come up roses – or runner beans!

Oxford Mail 6 March 1980

I returned to the subject in 1991.

Going green

No matter how humble the funeral, you can't have mourners issuing from the crematorium chapel to see a black cloud billowing into the air or the smell of burning plastic dominating the inspection of the wreaths. Even if the adults pretended not to notice, sooner or later some inquisitive youngster would be bound to puncture the solemnity of the occasion by asking: 'Dad, is that grandma's soul going up to heaven? Does that pong mean she's...'

The increasing use of manmade materials has made undertakers sensitive to what you might call the functional impact of their trade. Now the growing interest in all things green is forcing them to think about its environmental effect. The National Association of Funeral Directors is holding a one-day conference in Birmingham on March 5 at which, it tells members: 'Leading industry voices will discuss how environmental issues will affect your business in 1991.'

The reason for the gathering, said Oxford funeral director Mike Duckworth, who represented local undertakers on the Association's national executive, was the new Environment Protection Act covering everything from car exhausts to river pollution. From April emissions from all new crematoria in Britain would have to fall within the limits the Act specified.

As there were no crematoria under construction, the real purpose of the get-together was to prepare funeral directors to meet the requirements of the Act and the barrage of questions they were bound to face from their customers in the years ahead. While nobody in Oxfordshire so far as Mr Duckworth knew had yet asked for a 'green' funeral, the day was not far off when environmentally conscious relatives would want to know: if they had granny cremated, could they be sure she would not punch another hole in the ozone layer on her way to meet her maker? Or, supposing they buried her, could they rest assured she would not pollute the earth for her grandchildren?

'Until somebody does some detailed research,' confessed Mr Duckworth ruefully, 'it is not going to be easy to provide satisfactory answers. Although the Government has laid down the limits within which we must work, its pollution experts haven't given us any firm guidance on how to achieve them. All the Act says is that it's up to local council environmental health officers to enforce them, and if any crematorium built after April 1 fails the test, they can close it.'

Hence the presence in the chair at the conference of Les E. Baker, technical director of Rechem International Ltd. and chairman of the National Association of Waste Disposal Contractors. Hence the appearance on the panel of speakers with Peter Wilson, secretary of the Federation of British Cremation Authorities, and Brian Wilde, director of Britain and Europe's biggest firm of coffin furniture manufacturers, of Mike Bartlett, a hazardous waste consultant. Hardhearted as it might seem, our earthly remains are so much potentially hazardous waste.

The fact that almost two-thirds of us now opted for cremation had led funeral directors to adopt for functional reasons quite a few materials that they hoped would prove environmentally friendly too. Most coffins were made out of special Belgian chipboard that did not give off a lot of noxious fumes as it burned. Most had plastic fittings and linings made with the same purpose in mind.

But until somebody conducted experiments nobody knew for certain whether the emissions which they produced fell inside the limits laid down by the Act or whether other potentially noxious substances like embalming fluid would push them over the top.

Mr Duckworth said: 'The civil servants advise against the use of chipboard because of the bonding resin in it, but apart from the effect a ban on chipboard would have on the cost of funerals, I can't see where we'd get all the wood we'd need. Since Dutch Elm disease deprived us of our traditional source of wood, most of the hardwood we use has come from Malaysia, where it is grown under strictly controlled conditions.'

No environmentally conscious coffin-maker would dream of using timber from the rain forests. So, ultimately, we could end up having to rethink our whole approach to the disposal of the dear departed. One thing is certain. My hopes of coming up roses or runner beans in my back garden have gone forever. To whom it may concern, change of plan. Please will you scatter my ashes under the fig tree.

Oxford Mail 28 February 1991

Since then, of course, burials in wicker coffins in woodland cemeteries have become the preferred second option, meaning I can once again elect gratefully for burial and like Wordsworth's Lucy be 'rolled around in earth's diurnal course with rocks and stones and trees!'

Nuclear whitewash

It was with some surprise I read that Willie Whitelaw was recommending us all to whitewash our windows in the event of a nuclear attack. It is not that I disbelieved the Home Secretary. If he said it would provide effective protection against fires resulting from the heat flash of nuclear explosions, then it probably would. A chap with such an honest, lugubrious face would hardly tell a fib.

It's the recommendation to use whitewash that perturbs me. Somewhere in the loft I still have a couple of half-gallon cans of pale cream distemper. Bloomsbury Paste I think they call the stuff, which tells you how old it is. But does anybody still use whitewash? I thought it was superseded by emulsion paint years ago. 'That's right, sir,' a chap in the paint department of the [*now vanished*] builders' merchants, Stephenson's, told me cheerfully. 'Our cement department does still stock it in large drums for doing out cowsheds and that type of thing, but I don't think they sell a lot.'

Which makes me think. Supposing Jack Carter was fiddling with his dad the American President Jimmy Carter's nuclear buttons one afternoon in the Pentagon and he accidentally started a fullscale alert.

I rush home to find a queue a mile long outside the village's do-it-yourself shop and the proprietor out the back brewing up a foul-smelling concoction of lime, size and water in a brand-new dustbin perched on a rickety Primus stove. My wife is on the phone to Whitehall saying for the umpteenth time to a wilting civil servant: 'But if you work for Mr Whitelaw you must know. Will Woolworth's white emulsion do just as well or will it peel off in the heat?' And up the street old Jim Evans is battering his windows with a mixture of flour and water and confiding happily to his dog, Cindy: 'I don't know about protection, but if it's as hot as they say it's going to be we should get some damned good pancakes for supper tonight!'

Panic is the last thing we want in a crisis that could result in the extermination of a large proportion of the human race, but panic is what we are going to get if the powers that be insist on feeding us half-baked information.

I am just old enough to remember the start of the Second World War. As far as I can recall we were reasonably well prepared for that. We'd all got gas masks. We'd all decorated our windows in pretty patterns with brown paper sticky tape to prevent splinters of glass flying around in the event of a bomb dropping. We'd all bought yards of blackout material to hide the presence of our homes from the enemy bombers, although quite a few of us had forgotten that in addition to shining out of our front windows our lights also shone out of the back.

But when the first air raid siren sounded pandemonium reigned at Ten Mark Road, Headington. My mother disappeared in a puff of blue smoke. Before we knew where we were we were all sitting round in our gas masks and the cat, who had chanced on this scene of domestic bliss, was quivering with fright at the top of our neighbour's apple tree. Just imagine what it would be like if we all thought we might be dead in a couple of hours or – worse – that radioactive fallout would turn us into living corpses doomed to wander blindly across a devastated landscape until we collapsed in excruciating pain.

I must confess that in moments of pessimism I have toyed with the idea of trying to locate the filled-in cellar they say is somewhere under the living room floor of my cottage and kitting it out as a nuclear shelter on the Swiss or Swedish model. But that is a purely selfish gesture. What we clearly need is a National Day of Practice, a mock nuclear alert, what you might call a Sprung Bank Holiday.

One day when MPs are giving premier Mrs Thatcher a lot of stick during Question Time, the Chancellor Sir Geoffrey Howe is going to have to announce inflation has reached forty per cent, the Secretary of State for Industry Sir Keith Joseph is steeling himself to tell us half the nation is out of work, or there is the threat of another all-night sitting, Mr Whitelaw will rise to his feet and announce Operation Whitewash.

It will be the signal for the half of the nation still working to down tools, public transport to stop running, television and radio to fade out their regular programmes and all of us to prepare for the arrival of the fictional missiles.

There will be those of us who feel life simply wouldn't be worth living in a post-nuclear society. They will feed their children chocolate buttons and say: 'I don't want to hear another word out of you today – you're supposed to be dead!' The rest of us will spend our time trying to cope without gas, water and electricity and practising the various suggestions the Ecology Party list in their booklet, *How to Survive the Nuclear Age*, which they claim to have come from secret Home Office circulars.

It might be a bit much to ask grandpa to wrap his head in his jacket or grandma to do herself up in a brown paper parcel, but that is no reason why we should rail against those rich enough to have forked out £10,000 for a builder to install them a nuclear bunker with all mod cons, or those smart enough to have bought the necessary gubbins for £1,400 and done it themselves.

Between the sounding of the nuclear attack warning and

the arrival of the missile, says the leaflet, it should be possible to build an anti-blast lean-to out of heavy tables, bedsprings, doors and planks and lag it with mattresses. Then, after you've fished the dead rat out of the water butt and made yourself a cup of tea on the spirit stove, you can have a go at the second part of the exercise, constructing an emergency fallout shelter in the thirty minutes after the explosion before the radioactive downpour begins.

If you've got a cellar and it hasn't been filled in like mine, then you're lucky. You can build your shelter in there. Otherwise choose a spot well away from the windows and make a small den for your family out of chests of drawers, desks, work benches, or any other solid furniture. Take the doors to your rooms off their hinges and roof it with those. Then knock down the patio wall and place the concrete blocks on top, fill drawers with sand and use them instead, or cover your makeshift roof with copies of *Encyclopaedia Britannica*.

Who says a little knowledge is a dangerous thing? If the thought of spending a day humping the furniture round the house doesn't appeal to you – remember it's only a mock attack: you'll have to put it all back again afterwards! – then you could spend your time looking for culverts or exploring your local sewage system.

Culverts will only protect you from the initial blast wave or heat flash, but it's nice to know where they are, just in case you're taken short by a nuclear bomb while out walking in the fields, and dropping down a manhole will at least give you the experience of breathing contaminated air.

At the end of the day the top national and local

'And 78 gallons of whitewash, please' (Jim Needle cartoon)

government officials, who are supposed to run the country in the event of a nuclear attack, will come out of their subterranean fastnesses and see how we've made out. The Oxfordshire Rural Community Council will award prizes for the best prepared villages and the most ingenious fallout shelters.

The Army will rescue any of us whose efforts have collapsed on top of us. The Fire Brigade will flush out any who have got stuck down sewer pipes, and in the final analysis if the whole thing turns out to have been a complete cock-up from start to finish? Well, never mind. Just think how shiny our windows will look after we've scrubbed all that whitewash off!

Oxford Mail 16 August 1980

Flogging off Britain

Ever since the estate agents, Knight, Frank and Rutley, put Salperton on the market a few weeks ago, I have been wondering a little eerily what it is like to be up for sale. There aren't many places left like the tiny Cotswold village between Stow-on-the-Wold and Cheltenham which are still in private ownership. Great Barrington and Great Tew are the only ones I can think of in the Oxford area.

But supposing Mrs Thatcher decided to sell off bits of Great Britain in the same way she is disposing of the Post Office and other nationalised industries? Supposing the Tories on Oxfordshire County Council decided they'd had enough of the Liberal rump in Eynsham wittering on about gravel extraction, that most profitable sector of private industry? Supposing West Oxfordshire District Council have concluded that the only way they will ever be able to get the cash to implement their modest proposals for the future of my village, the Eynsham Local Plan, is to flog it to some rich Arab?

As a candidate for estate agents' hyperbole perhaps the place is not quite in the same league as Woodstock, Burford and Dorchester, but an aspiring copywriter could shut their eyes and do a fairly good job. 'Seat of the monks, this desirable, compact village of some 5,000 souls on the bank of the Thames has been a place of settlement since Saxon times and possibly earlier. Thriving community with own health centre, schools, post office, baker, butcher and numerous other shops. Pretty market square dominated by ancient church. Large conservation area. Secluded car park. Convenient to M40 and Oxford. Offers in excess of...'

It is the thought of what oriental potentates such an advertisement in the Middle East equivalent of *Exchange and Mart* might bring to Eynsham that disturbs me and even more the prognostication of how the village might greet them.

In the days of the monks the Lord Abbot might just have got away with telling the local peasantry: 'Comb your hair and do your flies up. Duke Humphrey is coming tomorrow!' Today what underling below the grade of Permanent Private Secretary to the Department of the Environment would risk going round exhorting the natives to paint their gutters and clean their windows? And what reception would he receive? The mind boggles at the obstructions a determined community might place in the way of any attempt to dispose of them to the highest bidder.

For the sake of argument however, let us pretend that those wizards of the property world, the Crown agents, have successfully surmounted all the obstacles. Having discovered the chairman of Eynsham Parish Council is a woman, His Divine Holiness, Shree Pramukh Swami, has conveniently gathered Swinford Bridge might collapse under the weight of his elephant and abandoned plans to turn the village into a retreat.

The Ayatollah Khomeini has learnt that there are eight hostelries and one club, not to mention an off-licence, all dispensing noxious liquors, and has decided it is not on to cut off half the villagers' right hands, pint glasses in them. Only one oil-rich Sheik remains still toying with the idea of establishing an oasis of Islamic culture in the Upper Thames Valley. He is coming to inspect the site for himself.

There is one embarrassing moment at the toll-bridge when the attendant refuses to let his chauffeur-driven Rolls through for nothing and solemnly gives him change of the eventually proffered £100 in two ps, and another when he steps from his car onto a dog turd which some unthinking peasant's hound has deposited at the last minute on the carefully scrubbed pavement. But a gallant member of the Royal British Legion Women's Section has carefully cleaned the soiled slipper.

An equally obliging member of the W.I. has proffered a cup of tea which his Serene Highness is sipping with an inscrutable smile, and the doubting and deserving of Eynsham are queuing up to present their petitions.

There is the Vicar, flanked by the stalwarts of the St. Leonard's Appeal Committee, hoping the potential owner of the village might see his way to making a £100,000 donation to the church restoration fund not, as malicious rumour has it, converting the crumbling edifice into a mosque.

There is a small knot of parish councillors anxious to persuade him to buy the Government Surplus warehouse and transform it into a community centre with, say, morris dancing on Tuesday and belly dancing on Thursdays.

There is a consortium of developers who would like to erect a superstore on the site of the British Leyland Depot with boating marina, lido, 500-acre tourist caravan park, 350 houses and, as a sop to the community, a skating rink on a disused gravel pit adjoining the A40.

Bringing up the rear there is the usual motley crew with individual grievances from the motor engineer who wants His Serene Highness to cut through the red tape that has prevented him opening a garage – perhaps he suggests hopefully it could serve the Sheik's own brand of oil and petrol – to a forlorn village elder wanting to enlist his help in saving a footpath.

His Serene Highness listens carefully to what they have to say, or appears to. He politely declines the suggested per-ambulation of the parish boundaries and the offer of lunch from the Chinese takeaway. Then he sets off in his Rolls to Eynsham Hall, which the by this time somewhat harassed estate agent points out is conveniently situated the other side of the A40 in large secluded grounds away from the peasants.

For the first time the Sheik's eyes light up when he sees the parade of cadets that have been lined up in honour of his visit in front of what was until recently the Police Train-ing Centre. The mod cons of the nearest Eynsham can offer to a stately home don't concern him much. After all, there is nothing wrong with the place that a few billions won't put right. But the prospect of a private army with uniforms appeals enormously.

The estate agent swallows hard and tries to explain. These young men are bespoke, so to speak, but with the soaring rate of unemployment he is sure His Serene High-ness would have no difficulty recruiting his own retinue. It is to no avail. The Sheik has lost interest.

'What is this Kidlington?' he demands. 'Your brochure claims it is the largest village in England.' The dumbfounded look on the estate agent's face speaks volumes. 'Very well then, what about Woodstock?'

The estate agent's face brightens and he launches into a paean extolling Blenheim Palace, the historic pile of the Dukes of Marlborough, the landscaped park designed by Capability Brown, Vanbrugh's architecture, his golden balls gleaming in the sunlight. A sidekick taps him on the shoulder and whispers discreetly in his ear: 'Hold your horses, Benedict. What's he going to say when he discovers he'll have coach loads of tourists every afternoon tramping through his front room?'

Oxford Mail 29 July 1980

The Eynsham references were all hot topics at the time. Vanbrugh's golden balls was a phrase coined by a famously naive Oxford Times women's editor. Its sub-editors kept a book of the howlers they had had to take their blue pencil to. The chief reporter at our Abingdon office perpetrated another by writing the town was to introduce do-it-yourself toilets. He meant they would not have attendants!

The Wanderer

The pull-out weekend entertainment supplement's first issue of 1981 featured a picture by my wife, Sue, of me carving the turkey watched by our daughters, Katie, Anna and her Christmas present, an outsized stuffed dog

218

she had christened Sindy Digby Chapman. The inspiration for the article beside it was some lines that had haunted me since I first read them as an undergraduate.

One of the oldest poems in the English language is about absent friends. The anonymous author of *The Wanderer* penned his 100-odd lines of Anglo-Saxon verse* well over a thousand years ago, but there is no mistaking the basic sentiment. The poor chap was fed up and far from home.

The poem might have been written yesterday by a shipwrecked sailor, who wandered down to the beach of his desert island and discovered the tide had washed up an empty beer bottle. He could be remembering the happy nights he spent in his local pub.

The poet recalls the fun he used to have in the banqueting hall before his master died and, in his mind's eye, imagines he greets again the kinsmen with whom he shared those festive occasions. Then he awakes from his daydream to the cold waves, the seabirds preening themselves and the snow tumbling down out of a leaden sky.

A lot of people feel like that at Christmastime. Suicidal 'wanderers' jam the switchboards of the Samaritans with pleas for help and thousands more feel impelled like turtles to return to their native hearth.

---

* I loved Anglo-Saxon. While some of my contemporaries struggled, for me it was another language after Latin and Greek on which to hone my skills as a translator. That no doubt was why I enjoyed a more cordial relationship with our tutor, Christopher Tolkien – later literary executor of his father, J. R. R. Tolkien – who also supervised my study of Middle English.

Often the feeling doesn't last very long. Battered wives who go back to their families with pangs of guilt remember in the bruised light of Boxing Day why they left home and, after the festivities are over, charities like Shelter spend the money they raised from Christmas appeals dealing with the dramatic increase in the homeless.

Whatever we like to think, a great many of us don't get on that well with our own kith and kin. However sincerely we sing about holy infants born in lowly cattle sheds, we have to face up to the fact that today there are more destitute people in the world than ever before. Those of us who do enjoy Christmas can count ourselves lucky. But unless we attach great religious significance to the festival it is very difficult to understand why.

My mother took me by surprise a couple of weeks ago by announcing a little sadly that it was the first time since I was born that she would not be seeing me at some stage in the holiday period. A couple of hours later my mother-in-law startled me when she rang up from Scotland to announce she had just iced her first Christmas cake for thirty years – a task my wife Sue has traditionally performed in the past.

But when I tried to recall the forty-seven Christmases I had spent at home, I found it almost impossible to penetrate the haze of roast turkey, sprouts, roast potatoes, stuffing, brandy butter and Christmas pudding. I have vague memories of eating cold ham and real pineapple for breakfast at my grandparents before the Second World War. But the first Christmas I can confidently remember is the year my sister Betty and I found out about Father

Christmas and brought the wardrobe down on top of us in our efforts to find out what was on top.

Subsequent memories follow the same peripheral pattern. Walking backwards and forwards to St. Aldate's Church in the centre of Oxford for a seemingly endless succession of services in the days when I was a choirboy. Stuffing my cassock pocket with diapers to mop up after whichever of the hundreds of communicants dropped the chalice at midnight mass when I was a server.

Sitting on my suitcase in the corridor of a packed train travelling home from Yorkshire on Christmas Eve, lying flat out in an empty compartment travelling north again on Boxing Night the year I entered journalism.

Watching the first snowflakes spin slowly down as I walked from the New Theatre to an ice cold office to write my pantomime review at the beginning of the severe winter of 1962–3. Perhaps most bizarre of all, sharing a Witney laundrette with an American serviceman on Christmas Morning the year we got married – wrapping our presents in between doing our washing – before going off to my first Christmas dinner with Sue's parents.

I have no doubt the meal my mother-in-law served up was excellent. But my memory of it has faded. Did we listen to the Queen's speech or did we switch on too late as usual? Was it that year I got backache from sitting in a cold draught watching ballet on television or was it another year? I've forgotten.

Part of the joy of Christmas I suspect is that however much it may seem to change it is always the same. When you are a child there is always an apple or an orange at the bottom of your stocking. When you grow up Aunt Edna gives you talcum powder or socks.

That's probably what makes it so hard for the 'wanderers' who come home after years of absence to enter into the spirit of things. They've forgotten the rules of the seasonal ritual. They are no longer paid-up members of the family. They are Christmas visitors and Christmas visitors – like cold turkey – begin to lose their appeal after a couple of days.

This year by accident rather than design we spent Christmas on our own for the first time. Apart from sallying out on Christmas afternoon to visit my wife's brother and his family, we observed our ritual alone.

What will I remember about the occasion? Trying to carve the turkey with Cindy Digby Chapman – my younger daughter's outsize canine Christmas present – at my elbow? Reviewing *Time and Time Again* at the Playhouse on Boxing Afternoon? Walking along the canal bank from Thrupp to the Rock of Gibraltar on Saturday? Or will it all blur and merge into other Christmases?

So long as I don't wake to the cold waves, the seabirds preening themselves and the snow tumbling down out of a leaden sky I shall forget gratefully.

Oxford Mail 3 January 1981

13 – Senior feature writer and arts editor

In the winter of 1982 Eddie Duller, who had succeeded Terry Page as editor in May, said to me: 'Don, just pop over to RAF Brize Norton, will you, and do a quick feature on their involvement.' Four days later I returned with six bulging notebooks.

It turned out the base had been engaged in every stage of the Falklands Campaign from the beginning to the end. It not only resulted in four full-page features. A few months later it earned me an invitation to become one the first quartet of journalists the Ministry of Defence flew to Ascension Island to take a detailed look at the RAF staging post to the islands in the South Atlantic. Even more fortunate was the commission in 1984 to compile the supplement to mark the fortieth anniversary of the D-Day landings in 1944. When Ralph Brain was news editor he liked to boast: 'Every story has an Oxford angle.' It was certainly the case with D-Day. One lead seemed to lead to another.

In November the same year I celebrated the twentieth

birthday of the column with a Jim Needle cartoon, but a few months later it was quietly dropped. Despite the paper's apparent prosperity, the change in people's reading habits and the continuing expansion in new forms of media meant it was having to fight harder for advertising and look at ways of cutting costs. I was appointed arts editor, a polite term that disguised the fact that in addition to covering the theatre I was now responsible for compiling the listings for the cinemas, museums and art galleries, and writing a weekly column about their activities.

Thankfully, Oxford being Oxford, I could rely on the expertise of a host of experts like Nicholas Penney at the Ashmolean Museum and Joan Crossley Holland at the Oxford Gallery, all grateful to have someone write sympathetically about their activities for a lay readership.

Turtle hunting on Ascension Island

When you go turtle hunting on Ascension Island, they advise you to stay well above the water line. The reason they give is the treacherous undertow and the freak waves it produces.

One minute you can be paddling your feet in the briny. The next a thirty-foot wave has leapt up the beach and grabbed you. You are speeding across the Atlantic Ocean – and if that happens, as Group Captain Anthony Mumford, the Commander of British Forces, put it succinctly: 'It is first stop Brazil.' Fifteen St. Helenans had gone that way in the past fifteen years and four RAF personnel had nearly followed them in the last four months.

But the turbulent waters don't seem to bother the turtles. Between January and April these armour-plated amphibians arrive, haul themselves up the beach, lay their eggs in the sand, then set off home again to South America.

There is something bizarre about a turtle hunt. You spill out of the Exiles Club about midnight sufficiently inebriated not to mind the short but bumpy journey by Land Rover from Georgetown to Deadman's Beach. Then you pile out into the warmth of a tropical night and set off on foot into the darkness.

To the left of you the sea keeps up its relentless pounding. To the right are the dunes into which the turtles burrow to lay their eggs. Ahead hover the lights of the oil tankers in the harbour. The setting is so unreal that it would be no surprise if a freak thirty-foot wave suddenly deposited one of the 400lb creatures at your feet.

In fact, what you are looking for are turtle tracks and as your eyes become accustomed to the gloaming you begin to see them: great grooves up the beach with feathering at either side where the turtle has dug her flippers into the sand.

Some are old tracks which the waves have washed away lower down. Others double back to the sea, indicating the female turtle has sensed a hostile presence on the beach or decided the temperature of the sand is not right for her eggs. But sooner or later you find a track disappearing resolutely in the darkness, you follow it and if you are lucky you come upon a turtle determinedly digging her nest in the sand.

Until that moment a certain jokey hilarity has pervaded the expedition as the hunters stagger up and down the beach not sure what the hell they are supposed to be looking for and disappear with muffled oaths into abandoned turtle pits. Now – in the presence of the quarry – an awesome sobriety descends.

The old girl groans in the throes of her labour and tosses the occasional flipperful of sand out of her pit. She has all the weariness you would expect of a creature who has just swum all the way from Brazil to answer a call of nature.

It is impossible to tell whether she is preparing to lay her eggs or tidying up after the operation, unless you actually see the soft white golf-balls dropping into the sand. But you cannot help feeling you are in the presence of a mystery. For thousands of years, possibly millions, the powerful creature and her ancestors have been coming to Ascension.

Yet nobody knows for certain how they locate this tiny volcanic outcrop in the South Atlantic after their long journey from their feeding grounds off the South American coast – let alone how they manage to find the same beach. One serious-minded professor has actually suggested that they navigate their way there by the stars, another that the island has about it certain nuances of taste and smell to which the turtle is supersensitive.

Turtles are probably at their most vulnerable in the first few months of their life. Of the hundred or so babies no bigger than the palm of your hand who break from the nest after seventy days maybe only one will survive into adulthood. Those that the island's seabirds and wild cats don't pick off as they head pell-mell down the beach will almost certainly find their way into the jaws of a shark or some other predator of the deep.

But human beings also poses a threat to the adult turtle. At the police station I found a notice pointing out that under the Wildlife Protection (Ascension) Ordinance it was an offence to kill, injure or take turtle eggs. Do it once and it could cost you a £50 fine, it said. Do it more than once and you might have to spend three months in jail.

In theory life should have been a great deal easier for them in the conservation-conscious 1980s than it was in the food-conscious 1880s when they were captured by the thousand for their meat. In those days sailors waited on the beach for the turtles to finish laying, tipped them onto their backs so they couldn't return to the sea, strapped them by their flippers to barrels and towed them back to Georgetown.

There they languished in giant turtle ponds until the garrison cooks decided to serve turtle and chips again to the marines or one of Her Majesty's ships took on board a consignment. Now one of the jobs of the island's underworked police force was to count the number of fresh turtle tracks at dawn every morning so that the Governor could ban sightseers from the five nesting beaches if he thought they were preventing the females from laying.

As a result, Ascension Island was one of the largest and probably least molested turtle hatcheries in the world. But because of overexploitation elsewhere, the green turtle could still be in danger of extinction. People like the island's tame historian, John Packer, believed it was time there was a serious study of the threats to their survival.

One source of danger was the increasing pollution of the world's oceans. Another was the growth of the island's human population. More people meant more rubbish, and more rubbish meant more blackfish. Were these shallow water scavengers, who would eat anything from a crisp packet to a cigarette end, swallowing more baby turtles? Was there a need to revive the island's turtle ponds and keep the hatchlings there until they were bigger and better able to cope with the modern perils they faced on their ancient journey to Brazil?

Should we not perhaps have been cultivating these pre-historic creatures instead of marvelling at their survival into the twentieth century? It might be a bit much to suggest re-introducing turtle soup at the Lord Mayor of London's Banquet. After all these years the guests had probably lost the taste for it. But as a source of protein for the Third World, who knew? The prospects for a good turtle farmer on Ascension Island might be a great deal more promising than a good sheep farmer in the Falkland Isles.

Oxford Mail 11 April 1983

Privy secrets

My fellow journalists on the first Press trip to the Falk-land Isles staging post, Ascension Island, after the war bet me that I wouldn't get the picture below published, but I said I would – and I did!

When I was a small boy, I once used a dust closet in a house at Great Milton. After performing my ablutions, I depressed the handle and a sprinkle of dry ash slid down the pan and disappeared into the darkness. I was so fascinated I did it again. No more ash came. At the time it seemed as final as the burial service declaration: 'earth to earth, ashes to ashes, dust to dust…' though I can see now it was not.

The next person to use the closet probably lifted the lid of the dust hopper before sitting down, cursed as I do when my children use the last of the lavatory paper without replacing the roll, then set off to the kitchen for another shovelful of ash from the cinder tray under the Aga.

Loos and the antics people get up to in them have always fascinated me. I don't mean the sort of fantasy facts that might earn their incumbents an entry in the *Guinness Book of Records*…

Tolstoy corrected the whole of the seventh draft of *War and Peace* at a sitting, slipping the sheets under the door one by one to his wife… Coleridge had the inspiration for *Kubla Khan* in a public convenience at Porlock but was inadvertently surprised by the attendant asking him how much longer he was going to be and, in his confusion, flushed the second half of his poem down the loo.

No, I mean the mechanics of the operation. I can understand the desperate shortage of bumf that led the pioneers of the Wild West to hang mail order catalogues in their privies. What intrigues me is how they found satisfaction in those stiff glossy pages unless constant fingering had caused bio-degradation to set in or behinds were less sensitive when men rode horses. Imagine then, the mental contortions that ensued when I discovered that all the military facilities in Concertina City on Ascension Island were of the three-hole variety.

At the end of a twelve-hour flight in a properly flushed VC10 from RAF Brize Norton I had stumbled through the darkness of a tropical night to the W.C. block. I had awoken from my daze with a start when I pressed the button of the urinal and a noise like a mincer was followed by a swirl of evil-smelling blue liquid.

Then I noticed for the first time the canvas curtain beyond. The door opened as someone else came in for a pee. The sudden rush of air caused the curtain to lift momentarily and there revealed to my gaze were the three seats with their three toilet rolls and nothing you could call privacy in between.

In the interests of investigative reporting all four members of the Press used the three-seaters during our visit and on one hilarious occasion we took turns to pose side by side while the fourth member snapped us for posterity. But throughout the ninety hours we were on Ascension Island none of us saw more than one loo in use at the same time.

Sitting in solitary splendour at 3.30am one morning contemplating the revolution in social behaviour that had made an act private our forefathers would have found it quite natural to perform in concert, a disturbing thought struck me.

Supposing I was sandwiched between grandpa and

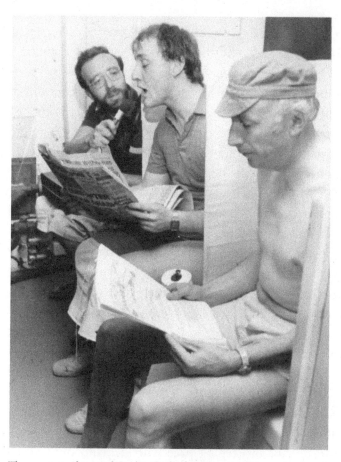

Three seats to the wind: Radio Oxford's *Peter Grant interviewing the* Bristol Evening Post's *Martin Powell while I peruse the local journal,* The Islander *(photograph Bob Lowrey)*

grandma, what would be the privy protocol? Would we be expected to sit there until grandfather reached the end of the chapter, put down his Bible and demanded: 'Boy, pass me the lavatory paper?' Would it be ladies first, eyes firmly fixed to the wall, three verses of *Onward Christian Soldiers* while grandmother adjusted the buttons of her combinations?

Or was there some Victorian variation on the three-point turn that enabled all three of us to rise in unison, paper over the cracks and resume our dignity without as much as cheek kissing cheek?

No one to whom I have put this fundamental question has been able to answer it. But I live in hope that my neighbour Mollie Harris may be able to satisfy my curiosity in her forthcoming book, *Cotswold Privies*, for which my wife, Sue, is taking the photographs.

In the meantime, perhaps I should report to the Ministry of Defence that the threefold thunder boxes they shipped out to Ascension Island at such vast expense are a complete – well almost complete – waste of money.

No one actually broadcasts the information, but one of Concertina City's worst kept secrets is that at the back of the American commissary where we had our meals there are two once gleaming modern, self-contained one-seater loos. The last time I visited one of them it was clearly suffering from overuse.

In despair of keeping pace with demand the staff had dumped a whole carton of lavatory paper outside the door. The cistern was suffering from metal fatigue. The waste pipe was almost totally blocked and when you flushed the lavatory the bowl spilled over onto the floor. Silly, I know, but I felt almost as sad as I did when the dust ran out in that house at Great Milton all those years ago.

Oxford Mail 27 June 1983

2020 vision

The George Orwell Professor of History returned from her day trip to the Falklands feeling distinctly restive. It was nice to see a few sheep again, but they were not the same woolly creatures Maggie Brown remembered grazing in Christ Church Meadow in her student days. As a wilderness Goose Green was not a patch on Otmoor.

Over breakfast in the Senior Common Room at St. Antony's College the following morning she felt so uneasy she almost voiced her fears to the Wykeham Professor of Computer Logic, but nine-year-old Sinclair Spectrum* was too young to know anything about female intuition or subliminal programming as he would call it.

She washed down her remaining food pills with the rest of her energising liquid, returned to her cubicle and tapped out the Bodleian Library code on her personal keyboard. She had done it several times since she got back from the suborbital space pad at Brize Norton, but the information remained the same. It was as she thought. Orwell had published *1984* in 1948. Some thirty-six years had elapsed between the creation of his dystopian vision of the future and its supposed realisation.

Tomorrow would be the first day of 2020 so another thirty-six years had passed since 1984. At least she thought it had. The Gregorian calendar no longer existed and even triple thinkers like herself found it difficult to carry out the

* The Spectrum launched in 1982 by Sinclair Research was one of the first British home computers. Clive Sinclair was later knighted for his services to British industry.

necessary calculations. After a certain point the universal computer simply refused to go on with the exercise. It erased the programme instructions from her screen with a self-satisfied: 'Task completed.'

For some illogical reason the approach of 2020 filled her with even greater alarm than she had felt at the prospect of 1984. It played on her mind despite all her efforts to persuade herself it was illogical: the product of a dis-eased mind.

She had piled into the electronic tube with the single-thinking proles and gone to Woodstock to see Barry Manilow at Blenheim. That was supposed to be the ultimate emotional depressant for an aged academic. It had certainly depressed her. The ecstatic androgynous faces around her seemed not to notice the plastic turf which covered the Park nor the paint peeling from the hardboard replica of the Palace.

Because they thought only what they were programmed to think they squealed with joy when the curly-headed retread of the famous singer dissolved into a big-boobed replica of Dolly Parton. It had sent a shiver down her spine. it reminded her of the Feminists' campaign against menstruation in the year 2000 that had resulted in test-tube babies and unisex adults with size thirty-two cups and uniform urinators.

She had risked the possibility of a random pre-programmed outbreak of hooliganism and joined the soccer special to the Maxwell Stadium at Horspath Road to watch Oxford United thrash Manchester United 2–1 in the Milk Cup. That was supposed to set the adrenalin of intellectuals flowing again and was much favoured by double-thinkers who found monitoring the proles' lives sickening or suffered mind-lag from servicing computers.

But didn't they realise it was merely a replay of the famous match in 1983 performed by specially programmed proles who would resume their places in the camps of contentment dotted around Oxfordshire tomorrow? Didn't they know similar famous sporting occasions were resurrected all over the world at regular intervals and in many cases like the Boat Race and the Olympic Games provided a regular diet for television?

They didn't. Unlike her they were incapable of three-dimensional thinking. They were unaware of the past or the future. They were plugged into an eternal present.

In a last attempt to unscramble her thought processes she had boarded the space shuttle and whizzed down to the Falklands. That was supposed to be the supreme deterrent for grey haired historians who longed for a glimpse of the real world. But instead of the cold, fresh air of Port Stanley penetrating her thermoplastic body protector and piercing her mind a stray shaft of sunlight had sent her brain racing back nostalgically to her childhood.

She could see again the trees waving in the breeze. King Alfred's statue in the market place. Wantage – the town where she was born – Wantage, the last victim of the Cold War that ended so abruptly in the 1990s.

The Americans and the Russians – or was it the Cubans and the Chinese? – had developed this laser-beamed nuclear rocket that was supposed to be the last thing in controlled long range weaponry. You clearly defined the limits of the target you wanted to hit, pointed it in the right direction, then pressed the button and two seconds later your enemy was left wondering where his key installation was.

Only some idiot behind the Iron Curtain had an epileptic fit during a training exercise and a couple of seconds later a team of bemused civil defence experts from Harwell were gazing into a black hole that bore a distinct resemblance to a map of Greenham Common* but alas was all that was left of Wantage.

That was the end of the generals, the air marshals and the admirals. That was the end of the politicians, the diplomats and the secret service. That was the end of the capitalists, the socialists and the economists.

That was the beginning of the computerised universe in which the message of the microchip was absolute. There was no need for the Spies, the Junior Anti-Sex League, the Thought Police or Big Brother. The computer programmed you into existence. It decided what you would think. It decided what you would learn. It decided when you would work, when you would rest, when you would exercise, when you would relax. It decided how long you would live and when you would cease to exist.

It was no use Maggie Brown having a brain scan. There was no chance of committing self-destruction that way. The machine could only cope with single-thinkers and

* Women established a peace camp at Greenham Common in September 1981 to protest at the storage of nuclear weapons at the American air base there. Despite vigorous opposition they did not dismantle it until 2000.

double thinkers. It was merely a way of checking they carried out their programmes properly. She would have to have a body scan.

She chose Entrance 1936, the year of her birth, to the John Radcliffe Health Centre and issued into a large comfortable room where an electronic organ was playing digital music. The room was filled with people suffering from various ailments who had come for a check-up. Most she knew would never emerge from the scanner. If it decided they were incurable or would cost the Health Service more than a few pounds to put them back on their feet again they would be, to use Orwell's word, vaporised.

As a geriatric who hadn't had a medical check-up for at least thirty years she told herself her chances of surviving a body scan were nil. She inserted the plastic identity disc she carried round her neck into the slot. Then she climbed into the chair on the conveyor belt and prepared to release the brake. Already she knew the scanner would have spotted the characters 3-D on her disc and be compiling a video obituary of her just in case. But she didn't care. For some unknown reason she simply couldn't face the year 2020.

Oxford Mail 31 December 1983

Pushkar comes in from the cold

My wife's Christmas present last year wasn't quite what she had in mind. Sue wanted an old-fashioned ginger moggie

Pushkar (photograph Sue Chapman)

with green eyes and I'm afraid Pushkar's are yellow, but there is no doubt they were meant for each other.

When the Oxford filmmaker, Lynne Fredlund, asked me if I knew anyone who wanted a kitten, I said no, thinking in my male chauvinist way that would be the end of it. But first our photographer forgot to pick up the film still she'd promised me. Then my daughters rang up out of the blue to ask for a lift home after some last-minute present buying, so on Christmas Eve all the Chapmans turned up on Lynne's doorstep in Jericho.

The result was inevitable. I drove home with the film still under my seat, Sue sat beside me with a tiny ball of fluff tucked firmly inside her coat, and Katie and Anna fell about in the back, trying to think of a suitable name for the latest addition to the family.

The diminutive tom, who eventually ended up bearing the name of the Indian town where Katie had nearly died of food poisoning the previous summer – blame my bizarre sense of humour for that – was petrified by all the palaver of Christmas. He hid under the bed and wouldn't come out for saucers of milk or fish, let alone to christen his dirt box.

Eventually, after the ritual wrapping of presents and stuffing of stockings we retired to bed, turned out the light and at two on Christmas morning were woken by a very small person in search of warmth. He slid between the sheets and began to purr like a sewing machine. Pushkar had come in from the cold.

In the first year of his life, he has had to suffer the ultimate indignity of most domestic cats – being 'itted'. He has succeeded in catching only one bird – we suspect because his mother didn't have time to teach him the finer points of hunting – and as a result of being the runt of the litter and golloping all his food no matter how big a bowlful you put down for him, he suffers from seemingly permanent indigestion and flatulence.

But teenage – in cat years! – vandal that he is, lying in wait for Sue in the bathroom, doing his best to reduce all my articles to confetti, we love him and tonight, after trailing it along the landing and killing it like a snake, he'll be hanging up his stocking like the rest of us, either that or, if he can lay claws on it, my mother-in-law's best angora hat!

Oxford Mail 24 December 1991

14 – Personal problems

Don't ask me how I feel

Friends have learnt not to ask me how I am. Instead of replying with cheerful monotony: 'I'm fine' or 'a bit Mondayish,' I now launch into an analysis of my state of health as portentous as a weather forecast. Some days I do feel fine. Some days I do feel Mondayish. Other days I feel like death warmed up.

Apart from a slightly above average trace of psittacosis in my blood, which colleagues attribute to chatting up too many parrots at the National Cage Bird Show last December, there is no apparent cause for my malaise. After a series of exhaustive medical checks, it was only the other week that a registrar at the Chest Clinic at the Churchill Hospital said rather hesitantly: 'I'm afraid you may have what they call post viral syndrome or M.E. The good news is there is nothing radically wrong with you. You will eventually get better. The bad news is it could take months or even years.'

The best-known example of post viral syndrome is

myalgic encephalomyelitis and to judge by the literature I have been reading from the M.E. Association founded in 1976 by a group of sufferers and now a registered charity I have a mild form. It occurs when a normal healthy person contracts a viral infection and for one reason or another appears not to recover fully from it – or, if they do, very slowly.

It has a number of severe symptoms including muscular fatigue, muscle pain, lethargy, exhaustion or a general feeling of being ill and not being able to perform the simplest of everyday tasks adequately. Although promising blood trials are going on at the moment, so far it has defied positive diagnosis.

Dr David Smith, the Association's medical adviser, told me there were probably more than 100,000 people in Great Britain with post viral syndrome but probably fewer than five per cent knew they had the disease. In any given year about one in every thousand of the population was likely to go down with it and their illness would last six months or more. In ninety per cent of cases they would shake off most of the symptoms within two years and, though the disease might linger on for years in the remaining ten per cent of cases, few would continue to be chronically ill.

Just as well, perhaps. Dr Smith said: 'To date there is no evidence that any therapeutic approach to the treatment of post viral syndrome is curative or that it reduces the length of the disease.' All doctors could do was offer a series of suggestions to 'maximise the possibility of spontaneous recovery.' Monitor yourself carefully. Avoid mental or physical effort that leaves you feeling like a limp rag a couple of days later. Steer clear of general anaesthetics, surgery and vaccinations if you can. Keep away from people with colds and other infections, and keep off antibiotics and alcohol if they upset you.

Fortunately, in my case my lunchtime pint of lager seems to have no ill effects. Though I was off work for seven weeks earlier in 1984, unlike some sufferers I had never been so disabled as to find it difficult to walk to the bathroom or make a cup of tea. My relapses had come from trying to do too much, though they had taken some maddening forms.

After ten days in Scotland working off and on in my mother-in-law's garden without ill effects, I spent three hours tidying up my mother's garden at Wood Farm and within a couple of days was under the weather again. Nor had I reached the state of mental exhaustion where some sufferers cannot take in what people are saying to them, though on bad days I did have difficulty concentrating and remembering things.

Like most sufferers, it was the psychological symptoms I found most disturbing. For no logical reason I would panic about things I should have been able to do standing on my head. During the press show of the latest James Bond film I suddenly broke out in a cold sweat: 'What on earth am I going to write about this?' I kept asking myself. I lost my self-confidence. I felt depressed about life. My mood changed without warning. I snapped at my wife and children for no reason.

I was lucky. Eynsham Health Centre and the Chest

Clinic treated me with unfailing care and sympathy. Other sufferers, it seems, have not been so fortunate. Their doctors do not recognise post-viral syndrome and have told them it is all in the mind.

Sprawled on the sofa, not being able to summon up the will to go and mow the lawn, I have accused myself of malingering. Panicking about how I am going to transfer a story from my notebook to the typewriter, I have wondered if I am losing my grip on life, heading for a nervous breakdown, succumbing to stress. That's the awful thing about having an illness for which there is no clinically identifiable proof. You can't even be sure why or if you don't feel well.

Oxford Mail 21 October 1987

M.E. was one of the reasons I took early retirement when it was offered to me in 1994. Ironically, I spent the first week without ill effects helping to pack up my mother-in-law's croft in Wester Ross before she moved to the house in Newland Street, Eynsham, where Sue and I now live, round the corner from our home for fifty years, Millstone Cottage.

There has been a lot of research into M.E., as the M.E. Association records in its authoritative quarterly journal, M.E. Essential, and experts worldwide know a lot more about the condition than they did when I interviewed Dr Smith, who in retrospect took a surprisingly optimistic view of the prospects for recovery. In fact, it continues to defy definitive diagnosis and, as the journal records, many people of all ages continue to suffer cruelly from it.

Apart from taking a term out when I was studying for the part-time doctorate, which led to the publication of my book, Oxford Playhouse: high and low drama in a university city in 2008, I have enjoyed a largely trouble-free retirement. Unlike most sufferers I am one of the fortunate five per cent who seem to have made a complete recovery. Sadly, not so in the case of my right ear!

Losing my balance

I got up to go into the surgery, staggered across the floor and narrowly avoided crashing into the doorpost. 'I know exactly what's the matter with you,' my doctor told me cheerfully. 'The same thing happened to me four years ago. I was sick all over a wall in Witney High Street and ended up hanging onto a lamppost, powerless to move. You've got...'

I have forgotten the name, if I ever registered it in my disorientated condition. But apparently an infection attacks your middle or inner ear, destroying your sense of balance. Your ear sends misleading signals to your brain and you end up thinking you're drunk. In other words, you get the after effects without the pleasure.

In my case my ear was clearly informing my brain I was looping the loop. My eyes were rotating like some unfortunate character in a Walt Disney cartoon. My doctor called his junior partner to come and have a look at them. 'I've never seen a case as bad as that before,' he said with satisfaction.

My wife, who comes from a medical family and therefore regards physicians with less awe than I do, was beginning to get alarmed. She had told the receptionist I was an emergency but… From her strategic vantage-point she had caught a glimpse of two doctors dashing through the door on which I had nearly brained myself, hotly pursued by a nurse with a syringe.

At that moment the nurse re-emerged, all smiles, to allay her fears and a few minutes later, after the injection had done its work, she was leading me gingerly back to the car. 'Poor Don,' chorused the staff. I must say that is one advantage of village health centres. You do get genuine solicitude when you fall into their clutches, not 'What's the matter with you then? Take these and if you're no better come back in a fortnight.'

All the same, it is not nice being unbalanced. Your mind tells you that you have a small blockage in your right ear and apart from that you are perfectly fit and well. Your body tells you that you are suffering something horrible. You don't feel like eating and every time you stagger along to the loo your legs threaten to fold under you and your head to drift off on its own.

In a way, I suppose, it is quite a salutary experience. I now know what it is like to be deaf in one ear and, believe me, cleaning your teeth or crunching your cornflakes in mono instead of stereo takes some getting used to. I now think I know what it is like to have morning sickness (though actually it is the nausea when my head hits the pillow at night that gives me greater problems).

I now also have some inkling of what it is like to lose the

coordination of your limbs. Even such simple basic operations as putting on a vest or having a bath involve constant logistical reappraisal. It is harder than you think to dry your feet without shaking your head.

As always though, when I am confined to bed, it is the more fantastical thoughts that dominate my daydreaming. What happened before two tablets three times a day relieved the symptoms of ailments like mine? Did whole communities fall about in the Middle Ages uttering prayers in each other's good ears to the Almighty to rid them of their affliction?

Or is it a modern phenomenon? No doubt it would be fairly easy to find out if I asked one of my daughters to fetch me the *Encyclopaedia Britannica*, but the information is never in the volume you expect and, anyway, my daydreams make more compulsive viewing.

Take astronauts, they're a breed of men and women that have given me pause more than once as I totter along to the bathroom. What does weightlessness do to *their* balance? What would happen if they didn't keep taking the tablets? It's all very well for the film industry to keep churning out those space odysseys. But is the real truth that out there beyond the galaxies are lots of little men with long ears all grimly hanging on to their sick buckets? Is that why they're green?

Oxford Mail 1 July 1985

The day of my attack I had a dizzy spell while shaving so infinitesimal I wasn't sure if it had happened or not. I drove to work at as usual, more unusually was writing a story for editions when the room began to revolve. I finished it, then said to the features editor: 'Very sorry, Jon. The room's spinning, I'm going to have to go home.' He rang my wife, Sue. She alerted the health centre and came in to fetch me.

It turned out it wasn't Menière's Disease or some other nasty ear infection. A few mornings later I was lying in bed with my good ear to the pillow when Sue asked me what I wanted for breakfast. No reply. I was no longer dizzy, but tests revealed I was completely deaf in my right ear. The health centre got me an emergency appointment at the Radcliffe Infirmary Ear, Nose and Throat Department...

Full of strange noises

I can't hear a thing out of my right ear at the moment. Nor do I expect I will again. But since I collapsed with vertigo in my local health centre, I have moved on to more august medical surroundings. In a last-ditch effort to restore my audio system from mono to stereo I am lying in the Dodds-Parker Ward at the Radcliffe Infirmary, Oxford.

For one half of every waking hour I breathe sterile hospital air, though to judge by the feel of my toes the chill breath of summer is filtering in somewhere from the outside world. For the other half I have a plastic mask over my face which pumps into my lungs a gas called carbogen – a heady carbon dioxide cocktail with an oxygen base:

ninety-five per cent O_2, five per cent CO_2 for those of you who did chemistry at school. I presume it is purely coincidental that there is a tank at the foot of my bed full of tropical fish who appear to be doing much the same thing!

During sleeping hours, I should relapse into an oxygenated torpor, but that is not as easy as it *sounds*, if I may use a word I am obviously going to have to think about more carefully in future. At night the ward is full of strange noises that remind ear patients that it also deals with nose and throat cases. Stertorous snores and hacking coughs puncture the small hours.

My wife suggests that I could easily switch off by burying my good ear in the pillow and leaving my bad ear exposed. Not so. For some strange reason the pillow or the mattress under it becomes a sort of echo chamber from which far below me but much magnified I can hear the sound of my neighbour's or my own respiratory system.

The single-glazed windows which are such an attractive feature of what used to be the Nuffield Maternity Home are no barrier to the traffic that thunders along Walton Street all night or to the occasional diesel train rushing across Port Meadow. The bell of St. Barnabas Church tells the hours by the quarter and – worst of all – somebody has left a tap on somewhere. At first, I thought the sound of water was intended as a stimulus to patients in another ward who had come in for plumbing repairs. In the more rational light of dawn I realised it came from the aquarium.

The carbogen is not to enable me to climb Everest in my dreams or to rescue crashed aircrafts' black boxes from the bottom of the ocean, even though Sue brought in my swimming trunks by mistake for a change of pants! Apparently, Prednisolone – the other last-ditch form of treatment I am having – might just possibly arrest the inflammation in my inner ear, if that's what I've got, in some mysterious, unexplained way.

The four little red tablets I have to swallow three times a day for seventy-two hours, then in gradually diminishing doses, are actually steroids, the drug some athletes risk their sex lives for in order to improve their performances. My doctor must have seen the look of horror that flickered across my face when she prescribed them. Yes, she said, it was a rather large dose, but not for long and it shouldn't harm me.

So here I am goodness knows how many little red steroid pills later in Dodds-Parker Ward at the Radcliffe Infirmary when I suddenly discover it is the FEMALE in-patients wing of the Ear, Nose and Throat Department! The Department is hosting an important three-day ENT conference and during that period is only taking emergency cases.

I am on my way home too. A second audio test reveals that the carbogen has at some frequencies prompted a slight response but not enough to make it worthwhile continuing with the treatment. A fail-safe X-ray has proved negative. I must not do anything strenuous while I continue taking the steroids. I must just sit back and wait while that most sophisticated and sensitive of computers, my brain, gently reprogrammes me to cope with the disability.

Already I have lost my nautical roll and in a few days'

time I should feel confident to face the world again, to pick up where I left off. There will be difficulties, of course – but I shall just have to *play them by ear*. Yes, I know. That's another phrase I'm going to have to drop from my repertoire of cliches!

Oxford Mail 5 July 1985

The consultant registrar who discharged me said: 'It sometimes happens. I think a virus has wiped out the nerve to your inner ear.' That's what I told everybody until some years later I got a call from daughter Katie, who by then was a medical student at Bart's.

'Daddy, daddy, daddy,' she informed me with great glee, 'we had a lecture on the inner ear today. The chap explained it was a tiny shell of bone and it was difficult to know what went on inside it. Occasionally people lost their hearing for no apparent reason. Usually, they told them they thought a virus had wiped out the nerve to the inner ear!'

Turning a deaf ear

The Wedgwood blue paint on the walls and the Wedgwood green curtains at the windows give Dodds-Parker Ward at the Radcliffe Infirmary a cool modern look. Anodised aluminium rails make it possible for the nurses to screen off the beds; the beds themselves and other fitments help to maintain the illusion.

It is only when you look a little more closely at the old-fashioned radiators and the elegant eight-feet-high windows with their iron frames and brass handles that you realise you are in an old building. What is normally the female in-patients wing of the Ear, Nose and Throat Department of Oxford's most venerable hospital used to be part of the Nuffield Maternity Home.

I was born there in 1933, as I discovered when my mother came to visit her newly deaf son. She sat by my bedside looking up and down the ward for what seemed an age, then she said to me: 'Do you know, Donald, I think this is the room where you were born!'

She remembers a great, gloomy ward with long rows of beds – and well she might. Although it must have seemed the last word in medical architecture when it first opened in 1931, it is now showing its age. If you look really closely at the cracked ceiling and the blistering plaster on the walls you realise there is a damp problem. The noise of workmen repairing the roof punctuated my three-day stay.

It is one indication of the difficulty the National Health Service faces in trying to maintain the quality and range of its medical services in even a well-endowed region like Oxford. The other signs of the crisis in the NHS are not so obvious unless you have to queue for a bed.

I was lucky – I was admitted straightaway as an emergency. In fact, if it's a long time since you were last in hospital, you might wonder what Social Services Secretary Norman Fowler is on about when he talks about improving efficiency. I was staggered by the change for the better since I was last a patient nearly twenty-five years ago.

The treatment is quick. Most people who come in for routine operations seem to be well enough to go home within forty-eight hours. The back-up of the nursing and ancillary staff is of the same high standard, and great thought and planning seem to have gone into every aspect of running the place from the administration of drugs to the printed menu with its multiple choice of good institutional food.

What is most impressive is the relaxed atmosphere. The daily regime is no longer as stiff as the starch on matron's collar. You get the same sympathetic consideration from everybody as if you were lying in bed at home.

I have to confess I was not really a suffering patient. Apart from the trauma of suddenly going deaf in my right ear I had more or less recovered from my bout of viral vertigo by the time I reached the ward. I also have to confess I was not in hospital when the system was under pressure.

Because of an important Ear, Nose and Throat Conference at the Radcliffe the Department was taking only emergencies. But it did mean I was fit enough to sit up and take notice of what was going on around me. It did mean there was time to chat to the nurses about the difficulties of managing on their pay and other topics dear to their hearts.

Looking round with the steely eye of the cost efficiency expert I came to the conclusion that if I was applying commercial yardsticks, the only saving I could make was the cost of my own treatment.

The doctor who examined me with such patience and

thoroughness told me gently that the chances of hearing again in my right ear were extremely remote. Yet she unhesitatingly recommended that I try the only method scientists have so far found to have an impact on this baffling affliction.

The cost of my three days in hospital, four cylinders of Carbogen gas, a course of steroids and a series of X-rays may not seem much compared with the thousands they spend on kidney and heart transplants. But it is a small indication of the dilemma at the heart of the NHS crisis.

Can we continue to afford to provide treatment which MIGHT save an ear or a life without considering the odds or the cost? Is the fact that in one or two cases in the past the treatment has proved successful enough justification for trying again? Or should they say to people like me: 'We could carry out a couple of successful sinus operations with the cash we are gambling on you.'

Should they then add: 'Sorry, it's not on. You'll just have to learn to live with one ear.' Or in the case of kidney and heart patients: 'Sorry, you'll just have to go away quietly and die.'

I have thought about it a lot since I entered hospital, but I am still unable to produce a rational response. Not only – like most people – do I find it abhorrent to apply commercial criteria to questions of health, but there is the nagging fear that if you start penny-pinching at the bedside – and of course it has already started at the frontiers of medical treatment – then it will not be long before it infects the whole system.

You just have to look at the story of the discovery and

development of penicillin to see how a line of research that seemed for years scientifically as well as financially questionable finally resulted in the medical breakthrough of the twentieth century. A drug that was first tried out on terminally ill patients went on to save hospital services all over the world hundreds of millions of pounds. We may have to revamp the National Service to meet the challenges of the twenty-first century, but we should not underestimate what we are about.

Oxford Mail 19 July 1985

15 – Pursued by parrots

Despite being rejected for military service I wrote an incredible number of stories about war during my career, through Anthony Wood was involved with more than one ex-serviceman's association as well as a lot of other community groups. I also wrote a lot of stories about birds.

Bristol Billy is no more

Bristol Billy is dead. After a lifetime berating the customers of various Oxford area hostelries, the celebrated Amazonian green parrot is no more – and perhaps fittingly he died a reformed character. One day last month he passed away peacefully at Kennington and the seven Dunn children, with whom he spent the last eight years of his life, laid him reverently to rest in their back garden and erected a tombstone saying: 'Poor Old Bill.'

Nobody knows how old he was, but he probably came to England in a sailor's luggage about the turn of the twentieth century. He arrived in Oxford at the start of the First World War and took up residence at the Albert Arms in St.

Ebbe's, where he was a great favourite with the customers, especially the late Aubrey Plested.

So, when the licensee, Mrs Wright, died she bequeathed Bristol Billy to the owner of the wholesale confectionery business round the corner. Aubrey in turn entrusted him to the late Dennis Organ. Later, however, he had second thoughts about whether Billy really enjoyed the clean fresh air of the riding stables at Wolvercote and persuaded Mr Organ to part with him to licensee Arthur Waller and it was with Mr Waller, first at the Cherwell Hotel at Cutteslowe, then at The Vine at Cumnor, that he lived out the rest of his pub life.

'Hello, you dirty old b*****!' was his favourite form of greeting and he knew other choice taproom epithets which he would unleash between boozy renderings of *Roll Out the Barrel* and *Cockles and Mussels* when he was in song. But the trouble was that along with his more endearing habits like mimicking the children playing on the lawn or the women's darts team he had less endearing ones like letting fly a hail of husks, sand and droppings at customers who upset him and squawking loudly at the crack of dawn to be fed.

As a result, Mr Waller sold him to the Cumnor garage proprietor, Jimmy French, and Mr French sold him to Graham Dunn, with whom he lived first at Abingdon, then Kennington, where he died on 14 April this year. Mrs Dunn said when they acquired him Bristol Billy had lost most of his feathers and looked like a plucked chicken. He was extremely spiteful and could give you a nasty peck with his beak, the result they assumed of long teasing by pub customers.

Gradually though he softened. To his repertoire of songs he added *Happy Birthday* – a ditty he heard often in a household of seven children – and though he retained his distinct distrust of men he used to allow Mr Dunn to wash him down with a syringe.

On one famous occasion he called a woman Mayor of Oxford a dirty old b***** and he saw no reason to change his greeting for a mere vicar. He had a strong dislike of the clergy and policemen. 'All coppers are b******s' was another of his favourite expressions.

But there was no doubt that he mellowed as he grew older. From how often he recited *Poor Old Bill* you could have been forgiven for thinking a fit of repentance had taken hold of him and most of the later sayings he picked up came from the children.

'We rather thought he was going to die,' said Mrs Dunn. 'He stopped squawking for his food in the morning and showed no interest in it, but it was still a shock to find him dead in his cage and of course it upset the children. I don't think we shall have another parrot. He was such a character it wouldn't be the same.'

Anthony Wood Column *Oxford Mail* 15 May 1974

The polite Harrods' parrot

The last time I interviewed a parrot he sidled along his perch and leered at me: 'Hello, you dirty old b*****r!' but that was Bristol Billy, that bird of doubtful origin, who for ten years was the taproom comic of The Vine at Cumnor. Pretty Polly Perkins, for the last nine years the belle of the bar at The White Hart at Wytham, was far more demure and ladylike, when I called to pay my respects.

She whistled politely to me, coyly hung upside down from the roof of her cage when my colleague, Johnny Johnson, tried to take her photograph, and only came down when the landlord, Dennis Williams, waved a cherry at her on a cocktail stick. What you might call real class.

But then she's not your common or jungle Amazonian bird, which some jaded mariner picked up in a disreputable South American bar and taught to swear in his cabin below deck on the long voyage home. Polly Perkins came from Harrods, was no doubt whisked across specially crated in a jet from her native West Africa and, after a suitable period in quarantine while the Pets Department sorted out her pedigree, was dispatched to Oxford by rail.

'My grandmother had a parrot in her pub,' said Norma Williams, 'and I'd always fancied one myself. But Dennis would never let me have one. Then one day, about a year after we came here, I went up to London shopping and in a rash moment I bought Polly.

When I came back and told him he thought I was joking, and he still thought I was joking when a telegram arrived three weeks later saying: "Your parrot has arrived at Oxford Station. Please collect it." He thought I'd sent it.'

But the telegram was no joke and after Dennis had got over the shock, he soon got to like Polly. She sat on her perch, whistling quietly to herself, and apart from muttering the name of the Williams's son or some other favoured customer, she hardly ever uttered a word except at closing time when she could be heard calling 'Come on, come on' in ladylike tones.

On 2 January 1973 the thirteen-year-old grey parrot with the red tail called 'Come on' for the last time at Wytham. After ten years at the hostelry Dennis and Norma were leaving – the last in a long line of husband-and-wife licensees – and handing over to a manager.

Dennis was an architectural student when the Second World War broke out, but after joining the Royal Norfolk Regiment, serving throughout the war in the Army and ending up a major in the King's African Rifles, he found he couldn't settle again to his studies. He entered the licensed trade and in fact came to Wytham from Bournemouth where he was a sales manager for Ind Coope, the brewery which owns The White Hart.

For a spell Polly went into retirement with him and his wife at Oakley, but not for long. The couple had bought the George and Dragon at Charlton-on-Otmoor, which has a stone dated 1691 in the north-east gable, and in May they hoped to reopen it as a free house.

'It will be,' said Dennis, 'a pubby pub and we hope Polly will feel perfectly at home there.' Certainly, she should do, for like The White Hart at Wytham it has a history. It was at The George and Dragon in 1830 that the Moor Men met to form the Otmoor Association, which led to the Otmoor Riots.

However, if by any chance the campaigners against the scheme to flood Otmoor and turn it into a reservoir should decide to take a leaf out of the history book and use the pub as their headquarters, I trust they will watch their language when they talk about the Water Resources Board.

Anthony Wood Column *Oxford Mail* 2 January 1973

The 1830 Otmoor Riots resulted from the enclosure of the 4,000 acres of common wetland on which residents of the surrounding villages grazed their cattle, sheep, horses, geese and ducks. The military were brought in to quell the riots and many rioters ended up in prison. The proposed reservoir was never built and another proposal in 1980 to route the M40 to Birmingham across it also failed. Since 1997 Otmoor has been an RSPB nature reserve.

Pretty polly is pretty dumb!

I've chatted up some dumb birds in my time, but the fifteen I met at the Birmingham Exhibition Centre take the sunflower seed. There they were, the elite of the country's talking parrots and cockatoos, all lined up with a dozen finalists from the budgerigar world at the National Exhibition of Cage Birds, and not a peep could we get out of any of them.

'I reckon he's been oversold by his agent,' muttered guest judge James Ellis, who plays the zoo keeper in the television series, *One by One*, prodding a silent budgie with his ballpoint. 'I've got thirteen unanswered hellos and twenty-five minutes of me wittering like a maniac,' wailed a radio reporter issuing from the Ladies waving the tape she had just played back to herself in the loo.

On paper the annual contest for the Polly Parrot Trophy and grand finale of the Trill Talking Budgie Quest looked a natural for a journalist with my experience of appraising theatrical performances and interviewing talking birds.

After all, didn't I excite the parrot that used to decorate the bar of *The Vine* at Cumnor to unrivalled heights – maybe I should say depths – of eloquence? Didn't I as a junior reporter thrill the whole of West Yorkshire with the tale of a missing budgerigar that could say its own name?

When I walked into the sitting room to record the happy outcome of that story, a distinctly scruffy ball of feathers called Joey flitted from his open cage, perched on my shoulder and proceeded to fill my notebook with nursery rhymes. A performance like that would have had the national and local press eating out of his seed-box at Birmingham.

Despite the combined efforts of the judges, officials and owners, not one of the birds on display seemed prepared to live up to the promise of his cue card. Scooby, the Mealy Amazon parrot from Welwyn Garden City, wasn't screaming: 'You need earplugs!' Billy Briggs, the pied cockatiel from Tenby, wasn't rasping: 'Show me your knickers!' Bill, the African Grey from Leeds Castle, wasn't even blowing his nose.

While James Ellis did his best to keep the disgruntled media entertained, champion budgerigar breeder and judge Joan Robinson Kuttner got on quietly with the business of sorting out the birds who could do their stuff from those who merely looked stuffed.

Eventually she decided Basil – pronounced Bay-sil – a yellow fronted Amazon parrot from Nuneaton had the edge on Cocky, a greater sulphur crested cockatoo from Herefordshire. 'You should have seen him first thing this morning. He did *The Charge of the Light Brigade* beautifully and danced it too.' Then she went on to award first prize in the budgerigar section to Boy Blue from Southend.

'Don't you think it's a bit much to expect the birds to give of their best when they're all sitting in their cages side by side?' I asked, thinking no self-respecting actor or actress would ever audition under such circumstances.

'Darned right you are,' snorted American Master Sergeant Wayne Greenberg from USAF Mildenhall, still smarting from the defeat of his African Grey, Peppy, who could say 'Good Morning' and 'Good Day' in Japanese as well as 'Hiya Pep!' and other greetings in American. 'If they want to judge what the birds can really do, I think they should make them appear one by one with their owners in a sound-proofed booth.'

In that sense the bird seed manufacturers who organised the Trill Talking Budgie Quest had arranged things better. The twelve finalists were the pick of a nation-wide contest, which involved their owners sending in recordings of their birds performing. But not even Trill had thought of laying on tapes or video-recordings for the media and the public, who in a few hours' time would be flocking to the show.

Having tried in vain to coax a couple of scarlet macaws who were merely there for decoration to say a few words to the *Oxford Mail*, photographer Steve Randall and I prepared to leave. As we did so a scantily-clad model with a

Me, James Ellis and champion talking parrot, Basil, keeping mum in his gilded cage (photograph Steve Randall)

white cockatoo on her arm appeared on the platform, presumably in a last-ditch effort to please the Page Three brigade.

'Hello, what's your name and what can you say?' I asked her. Funny, she seemed to have lost her tongue too.

Oxford Mail 12 December 1986

My concerned GP sent me to a number of distinguished physicians in search of an answer to my chronic fatigue. Not long after my visit to Birmingham I saw a professor of immunology at Oxford. The office fell about when one of his tests revealed a trace of psittacosis – often called parrot's disease! – in my bloodstream.

The Australian registrar who conducted the follow-up said: 'So what, everybody has. I think you've got what they call M.E.'. It was the first time anybody had made what proved to be a correct diagnosis.

Pig in a poke

'This little piggy went to market, this little piggy stayed at home, this little piggy had roast beef...' and this dirty great Berkshire pig refused to budge an inch for me at Cogges Farm Museum!

I like pigs. I think they are entertaining, intelligent creatures, not at all like the villains in George Orwell's *Animal Farm*, so when I heard that Bob Morris was teaching the Museum's ten-month-old pedigree Berkshire boar, Buster, how to walk properly in preparation for his debut in the show ring, I thought: 'That is something I must try.'

'Fine,' said Cogges curator Chris Page, 'come along. We'll have a party of ten and eleven-year-olds from Greenmere School, Didcot, following up their studies on the 1881 Census. 'They'll be able to help you.' They did too.

While I took a crash course in the finer points of pig control, they woke Buster up, fed and watered him and generally did their best to get a tired pig on a hot morning into an agreeable frame of mind.

How a pig performs in the ring is crucial to his chances of winning prizes. If he trots along freely with a smile on his face and a curl in his tail the judges are likely to concentrate on his finer points. If he runs amuck, they are more likely to focus on his bad points. Hence the importance breeders and exhibitors attach to teaching their pigs to walk properly.

There are two simple tutorial aids. One is a bat to bat him across his backside in a friendly fashion. To him it is the equivalent of a pat on the bum. The other is a board to hold alongside his head like a giant blinker. By pressing it gently against his cheek you are supposed to be able to steer him in the right direction.

Buster's lessons had been going well Chris assured us. He enjoyed going walkies. Our only problem was likely to be keeping up with him. Suitably alerted, the lads from Greenmere, dressed for the occasion in nineteenth century farmer's boy neckerchiefs and cords, stood by his ears and his tail – the only parts of a pig you can hang onto. I, in my twentieth century reach-me-down cardigan, brandished my board and bat like a matador's cloak and sword and gallantly prepared to stop several hundredweight of pork on the trotter terrorising Witney.

So much for theory. In practice Buster took one look at the open door of his sty and refused to go anywhere with an elderly pig-poker like me. I batted him with the bat. I boarded him with the board. Dredging the last elements of animal husbandry from my memory, I even blew down his nostrils in the classic Barbara Woodhouse fashion*. He simply blew back.

* Barbara Woodhouse was an Irish-born British dog trainer, author, horse trainer and television personality. Her 1980 television series Training Dogs the Woodhouse Way made her a household name.

Eventually Chris succeeded in coaxing him out into the yard and a by now thoroughly disgruntled Buster allowed me to resume my lesson in pig walking. I gave him several sharp whacks on the backside – and, I fear the lads from Greenmere several painful cracks on their fingers as they tried to push-start the ponderous beast.

When he did at last trot hesitantly forward, I thrust the board in his face and attempted to steer him in the direction of photographer Susie Barker's camera. He wasn't posing with a pig's ear like me if he could help it. He neatly tucked his snout under the bottom of the board and raised his head sharply, practically wrenching my arm out of its socket.

Ignominious end to pig poking (photograph Susie Barker)

In the end I gave up and Buster, realising he had won, allowed me to steer him back in the direction of his sty. The boys went off to saddle the carthorse. The crowd who had gathered to watch the fun melted. 'If you want to see him walking properly,' I shouted after them, 'you'd better come back on Sunday and see Bob Morris in action.' Bob, who is a Friend of Cogges Museum gave him a half-hour jog every Sunday.

'I can't understand it,' Chris said to the chap who was bolting the door of Buster's sty. 'He's usually such a long-suffering, agreeable pig.' 'Didn't you know?' said the pig-man with an evil grin. 'He's got a bit of a sore shoulder.

Betsy' – his three-year-old Berkshire sty-mate – 'gave him a bunt last night.' What can I say, Buster? I feel a real swine...

Oxford Mail 2 July 1986

Joan Crossley Holland

When the Oxford Gallery opened at twenty-three High Street in 1968 it was as if some long lost argosy had come to port. Sauntering down the High to my digs overlooking Christ Church Meadow I would peer down through those slanting spy holes at rich tapestries, jewels and pots and imagine great holds stuffed with rare and exotic treasures.

I now know differently. Once a month on Thursday afternoons a magical lethargy seizes Oxford's traffic wardens, another band of artists beach their battered cars on those unlovely yellow lines and stagger into the gallery with their booty.

Through the sea of polythene and wrapping paper Joan Crossley-Holland moves imperiously, appraising each object with a keen eye, supervising the mark-up and giving the final word to her staff on its display.

I am not sure how I should feel if I was some young hopeful discovering to her gaze the creation on which I had lavished so much effort. Her taste seems so impeccable, her knowledge of the creative processes so profound.

But, as a journalist trying to explain the abstractions of art and crafts to a lay readership, I have come to value her expert guidance, I have learnt to keep my ballpoint poised for the phrase that pierces artistic pretension.

It required courage and vision eighteen years ago to launch a gallery treating artists and crafts men and women as equals. It has required greater courage and determination to keep it afloat in a changing climate. As artistic horizons have widened, so – maddeningly – the financial storm clouds have gathered threatening to sweep Mrs Crossley-Holland's charmed barque away.

Oxford Gallery 68–86, a brochure to mark Mrs Crossley-Holland's retirement. The gallery has since closed.

A golden oldie

I am just coming into my prime according to a new national market survey. Never mind the grey hair, the bald patch and the fact that I can't see to cut my toenails any more without my specs. I've paid off my mortgage. In another four years I will – fingers crossed! – have waved goodbye to both my children.

In six-years' time, I will collect my company pension. I am one of a rising generation of what they call Golden Oldies, the people who can look forward to retirement in comparative affluence. While the colleagues who will step into my shoes struggle to make ends meet, I will have cash to spare.

No wonder advertisers, who have for years aimed their goods and services at younger people on the assumption that they are the big spenders, are trying to think of ways to encourage us to part with our money. Already there are nearly six million of us. Soon there will be a lot more – and we have an estimated £90 billion in our pockets.

Companies will have to approach what could be 'the largest and most affluent market in history' carefully. We Golden Oldies are extremely cautious in our spending habits, says Frank Fletcher, the research director of Mintel, the specialists who carried out *The Lifestyles of the Over-Fifties* survey.

Fewer than one in five of us splash out impulsively without thinking. Most of us do not borrow money and, though we use credit cards, we are careful to pay off our debts before we incur interest on them at the end of the month.

That's not to say we are stingy. We don't sit at home watching television or checking our bank balances. We enjoy a drink, though we prefer small country inns that serve good food to city centre pubs with loud music and games machines, and we're more likely to order bitter and sherry than lager or vodka.

Over half of us listen to music every day. We enjoy curling up with a good book. But we're just as happy pottering around the garden. While one in five of the population wouldn't be seen dead with a hoe, only one in ten over fifty-fives feel that way.

In Oxfordshire it is difficult to obtain statistics to back up the survey because most companies for obvious reasons don't ask their customers their ages. But all acknowledge the trend.

Sam Shrouder, Apollo Leisure's director of operations, said it has made a major contribution to the tremendous upsurge in business at Oxford's Apollo Theatre and the Oxford-based group's other theatres across the country. 'The sort of shows that might appeal to the over fifties – the big musical revivals and ballet and opera – seem to be better supported than ever. The number of grey heads in the audience is very noticeable.'

Peter McMullin had also noticed the number of older people coming into Blackwell's Music Shop. 'Some of them spend quite large sums of money regularly on recordings.'

At the department stores they are much in evidence too, but store managers have to adopt a more sophisticated approach. Most of us middle-aged Britons like to think of ourselves as young. So, although we like to be well-turned out and are considerably more conservative in our tastes than our sons and daughters, we don't take kindly to clothes aimed at the older man or more mature woman. The same goes for furnishings, glass, china, electrical appliances and cars.

It is in the field of holidays that the trend is most obvious. Our cautious spending habits mean we don't mind owning up to our age if it results in a pensioner's rail-card or free bus pass.

The survey shows that nearly a quarter of the over fifties take a winter break compared to less than a fifth of the rest of the population and a whole new holiday industry has grown up to cater for us. To take just one example, Thomson Holidays – voted best tour operator for the over fifty-fives by the travel agents in February – offered 87,000 holidays in twenty-seven different resorts in the winter of 1988/89. Customers taking advantage of their Young at Heart offers could go for three nights or eighty-four, and those of us lucky enough to be able to spend more than a month by the Mediterranean could find holidays at seven resorts starting at only £1.99 a day

Gail Booth, manageress of the Lewis Travel Bureau at Selfridge's store in Oxford, said the booming trade in winter holidays for people like me offset the drop in summer trade because of the increase in mortgage rates. 'Some of the offers have been unbelievable,' she sighed enviously. 'When I'm old enough, I look forward to jetting off for the winter myself.'

Not that cheapness is all. She pointed out many of us Golden Oldies prefer to blow part of our savings on a longer haul trip to somewhere more exotic. Chris Simmons, the manager of the Abingdon Travel Agency said: 'I haven't got the statistics to prove it, but it is my impression that the majority of the more expensive holidays go to your age group and the increase in volume is noticeable.'

With Britain facing a shrinking workforce in the 1990s, it could be that some employers will even start offering such holidays as an incentive to their older employees to keep working.

Aware of the drop in school-leavers coming onto the labour market, Chancellor of the Exchequer Nigel Lawson has already done his bit by abolishing the rule that capped what you could earn if you were a pensioner in his latest budget. Tesco's and Sainsbury's have adopted a national policy of recruiting over fifty-fives, and the same thing is happening locally.

'We were only talking about it at our staff meeting this morning,' said Catherine Barton, the manager of the Oxford Job Centre. 'Employers are showing much greater willingness to employ late fifties and early sixties and are being much more flexible about conditions. It tends to be a case of you tell me how many hours you can do and we'll see if we can fit you in.'

That may be cheering news for the not-so-golden Oldies made redundant in the last decade, but the survey says employers may have to offer much bigger incentives if they are to maintain staffing levels. The plain fact is over half of us over fifties are looking forward to or already enjoying retirement, and only a third of us would welcome the chance to continue working.

Oxford Mail 27 April 1989

Forward thinking

A piece based on a briefing from Peter Jones, Deputy Director of the Oxford University Transport Studies Unit.

Let's pretend the year is 2022 and I'm still working, not pushing up the daisies in Eynsham Churchyard. Being a feature writer, I operate from home nowadays. I only visit the office in Osney Mead when the editor of the *Oxford*

Telemail, your indispensable small screen guide to what's happening in Oxfordshire and the world, calls me in.

Today I have received the summons. I press a few keys on my domestic computer and Fred, the green-eyed monster in the corner we named after a beloved cat, purrs softly as he offers me my travel options.

I could go by boat. The water-bus leaves the Caribbean Cruiser Station down the road at 9.30am. There is a two-hourly service and – thanks to electronically operated locks – it runs to time. But I'm not sure I can stand hearing the pre-recorded commentary for tourists for the umpteenth time.

I could go by electro-bus. The service is frequent. I enjoy standing at the stop watching the vehicles moving closer to Eynsham on the digital display map that has replaced the timetables. It is fun seeing it forecast how long the bus will take to arrive and the number of seats available increasing and decreasing as people get off and on.

You can pick up useful tips from your fellow travellers. The principal topic of conversation at this time of day on the journey into Oxford is usually the best buys available at the various ring road supermarkets. The shoppers monitor the fluctuations in prices on their home screens as carefully as any broker does the Stock Exchange.

I could go by railbus. That service is frequent too and it is a good deal faster than electro-bus. But though it runs on a monorail alongside the road, it won't drop you anywhere. As a result of a successful campaign by the University and the Oxford Preservation Trust the nearest you can get to the city centre are the spur-line termini at the Station, the war memorial in St. Giles, the Plain or Folly Bridge.

In any case the editor wants me to take him in some tomato plants (the real reason I suspect for the conference!). I had better risk the black looks of my environmentally conscious neighbours and take the car.

Fred tells me there are no traffic snarl-ups on the route to Osney Mead this morning, then courteously reminds me of the tolls involved: it will cost me two Eurocents to cross Swinford Toll Bridge and ten Eurodollars if I drive beyond the Botley Road Park and Ride.

I check the battery of my car. There's enough power to get me to Osney and back. The automatic electronic service link-up with my local garage tells me all systems are go. I remember to change the RAC compact disc on my inboard car computer from the one we used three weeks ago to fetch my mother-in-law and dog from Wester Ross to the one labelled work.

The centre of Eynsham is now a traffic-free zone except for disabled drivers and essential delivery vans, ambulances, doctors, etc. – a fact represented in the escalating property prices!

I turn left from Millstone Cottage, thread my way through the traffic calming chicanes in Hanborough Road and join the Eynsham Bypass. Because of the screen of trees, I can no longer see the A40 dual carriageway, but if I could, I wouldn't be surprised to spot a motorist whizz by with his feet up reading Thomas Hardy's *Far from the Madding Crowd*.

These days when you reach a major trunk road, you slip your gear lever into automatic and the computer takes over. Cars travel bumper to bumper without risk of pileups even in fog.

I wait for a family of cyclists from the new car free town near Barnard Gate to pass. According to a recent report in the *Telemail* over eighty per cent of the residents there use bicycles as their main form of transport. Then I cross the cycle lane.

Although the bypass is quite busy, there is no risk of me running into anything at junctions or roundabouts. An infra-red sensor automatically overrides my directions in the event of traffic hazards.

At the toll bridge another roadside sensor automatically deducts two Eurocents from my car bank account. Further roadside sensors prevent me exceeding the speed limit driving through Farmoor. At Dean Court the programme on the compact disc in my inboard computer means I have to join the Cumnor Hill Bypass. I would anyway for the view of the dreaming spires, which this morning I share with a party of open top bus passengers.

I glance down at the A34 as I cross the flyover. Somebody has broken down and is swapping cars. It's on occasions like that you appreciate the bonuses of leasehold motoring. Always a friendly neighbourhood garage to supply you with a replacement.

As I join the slipway to the Botley Road, the roadside digital display board informs me Gloucester Green car park is already full and Westgate has only thirty-four places – it corrects itself, thirty-three – which will be gone by the time I reach the centre of Oxford. Better to park and ride. 'If I was going to the city centre, mate,' I find myself muttering,

'I would have booked myself a parking space in advance!'
'Only seventeen spaces left,' the display board replies.

As I pass the Park and Ride and enter Oxford's central traffic zone, automatically paying ten Eurodollars for the privilege, the telephone rings. It is the editor. He's halfway to London by hovertrain, flashing through Reading at 300mph. Would I leave the tomato plants in the boot of his car. He gives me the combination number.

What he wanted to talk to me about was a feature on Oxfordshire traffic in the popular Bad Old Days series. 'There must be plenty of suitable video clips in the County Archives at Woodstock and with your long memory... Hop over there and find me about thirty minutes-worth, would you?'

'Yes, and it might be fun to have a clip of a Keystone Kops car chase,' I say. 'Who are they?' he says. So much for twenty-first century whizz kids!

Oxford Mail 18 June 1990

Facing the knife

I have just achieved one of my long-held ambitions – to interview a knife-thrower at work. I must confess I wasn't as brave as the young lady at St. Giles's Fair years ago who – the fairground barker used to inform us – wore nothing to protect her body from the naked steel. Nor was I as pretty as Manya, the trusting wife at whom Adam Rudolf usually throws his knives.

Facing the knife

But at least I stood there, speechlessly trying to write down my impressions in my notebook while the star of the Hungarian State Circus made his points and emerged unscathed a few flashed-by seconds later with a blank page to show for his and my efforts.

Visit *Rubicus*, the celebration of circus arts in the heated Big Top next to Oxford Ice Rink for the next ten days and you can take Manya's place and risk an early release from your mortgage repayments, the gas bill, the Poll Tax and all of life's other little troubles.

John Roberts of Robert Brothers' Circus is fulfilling one of *his* long-held ambitions to present a new type of circus entertainment in the fifteen to twenty towns which —like Oxford – won't accept animals. It is the first travelling circus to have a licensed bar, craft stalls and a Chinese takeaway inside the Big Top and the first to carry a PG certificate on all its posters.

Having tucked his lions, elephants and horses up for the winter at Peterborough, John is taking to the road with a more sophisticated entertainment designed to appeal to people in search of a night out that's a little different. The doors open at seven each evening and for the next hour the audience is free to wander drinks in hand among the attractions. Then they settle down to watch a seventy-five-minute cabaret with dancing girls and some of the top circus acts in Europe.

Jugglers, who usually perform on horseback, will ride round the ring on dumper trucks. A high wire artist will finish his act by riding across a tightrope on a motorbike. And in place of the ringmaster comedian Mark Too, who will be playing Idle Jack in pantomime at Blackburn this Christmas, will whizz in and out in a crazy car.

John calls it *Rubicus* because 'like the Rubic Cube it's circus that is a bit of a puzzle', but he is hoping Oxford audiences will like it and, if they do, he's planning to tour Britain and Europe with it next year.

Oxford Mail 14 November 1991

Yellow Pages turn fiction to fact

Now that an enterprising publisher has satisfied public demand for that non-existent book, *Fly Fishing* by J R

Hartley, I hope a French polisher will set up shop in Brize Norton. Actor Norman Lumsden captured the hearts of the nation with his quest in the Yellow Pages television commercial for that out-of-print volume it turned out he had penned himself.

After watching it, thousands of viewers turned to their Yellow Pages, found the nearest booksellers in their area and asked if they'd got a copy.

So, I can't be the only one who reached for my Yellow Pages after watching that other commercial. You know the one. Actor Simon Schatsberger comes to life after a late-night party at his home and cleans the place up with the help of a girl he can't remember before his parents arrive home.

Suddenly he notices somebody's scratched the table and calls out a French polisher. 'Just landed, mum? I'm on my way to fetch you,' he sighs with relief as the craftsman finishes repairing the damage, only to notice as he puts the phone down somebody else has decorated a priceless picture with a moustache.

Well, I don't know whether you've noticed, but the entry he stops at when he's running his finger down the Yellow Pages for the French polisher bears a perfectly legible telephone number: Brize Norton...

It's no use trying to ring it. There is no French polisher at Brize Norton. If there was, he'd have a Carterton number. There is no Brize Norton exchange. Like *Fly Fishing* by J R Hartley, it is a figment of the scriptwriter's imagination. Or rather was.

Sitting on my desk as I write is a brand-new edition of the book that never was, published just in time for Christmas by Stanley Paul with delightfully nostalgic illustrations by Patrick Benson.

At the front J R Hartley, who has asserted his rights to authorship in accordance with the Copyright, Designs and Patents Act 1988, expresses his grateful thanks 'to my search-mates, Yellow Pages, to my publisher Roderick Bloomfield for revitalising the quest, to Peter Lapsley for appraising these memoirs with his expert angler's eye, and to Michael Russell for setting them down'.

The author has a nice dry sense of humour and his story has the innocent appeal of an old-fashioned schoolboy yarn. But I fear only anglers will be really hooked by the narrative. Even as a student at Oxford J R Hartley spends most of his time in the Cotswolds fishing for trout in the river Coln.

In fact, if Yellow Pages ever move on from poignant minidramas like saving the legs of clapped out gardeners by providing them with motorised lawnmowers, it could provide the inspiration for the perfect sponsored series, *Gone Fishing with J R Hartley in the Yellow Pages.*

In the meantime, about that French polisher. My wife is in Australia visiting her brothers and there's this antique desk of hers. I'm not sure how it happened. It might have been me or the cat or… but that's none of your business! I need a French polisher, not any old French polisher, the one at Brize Norton. So quick, so skilful, so discreet. I know he doesn't exist at the moment. I want to be first in the queue when he does!

Oxford Mail 21 November 1991

Living with death

We like to think we let it all hang out in today's world, but when it comes to death, we're a great deal more squeamish than our ancestors. Granny never dies. She passes away peacefully, leaves the world behind her, goes to a better place, joins her Maker. The hardest thing we can find it in our hearts to say is that she went suddenly, and that's not a criticism of the old dear. It merely means she took us by surprise.

Even in the pub when the relatives are not around, we tend to talk in euphemisms. 'Heard about old so-and-so? Popped off... kicked the bucket... handed in her Bingo card.' For well over a century we've done our best to wrap the fact that none of us has a return ticket in a shroud of mystery.

In 1991 Nigel Llewellyn and the staff of the Victoria & Albert Museum in London set out to demonstrate that earlier generations were more open about death. They not only surrounded themselves with objects that reminded them sooner or later they would die. They went out of their way to preserve relics that kept green the memory of the deaths of friends and relatives.

What happened? No sooner had Nigel and his chums assembled a display of deathly treasures from museums and churches all over the country than the Gulf War broke out. 'Dear, oh dear,' said the powers that be. 'What's this? *The Art of Death: Objects from the English Death Ritual 1500–1800*? We can't have that little lot cluttering up the V&A for the next three months. 'Supposing our brave lads

Lydia Dwight death bust

in the frontline start coming home in body bags? What would people think? We'd have apoplectic MPs standing up in the House of Commons demanding the Government chops our grant.'

A year later poor old Lenin's chances of receiving another dose of embalming fluid are not too bright and there are several other trouble spots where you take your life in your hands every time you cross the street. But now that things have calmed down on the home front the V&A

has been able to assemble its goodies again and, for the next nine weeks, they are on display at the museum in London, among them a number of choice exhibits from Oxford.

A death mask of Oliver Cromwell after he snuffed it in 1658, a painting of the antiquary John Tradescant on his deathbed in 1638, a bronze figurine of a corpse in a shroud, a chunk of wall painting depicting the Dance of Death and a watch in the shape of a skull – all from the Ashmolean Museum.

There's also Bishop Fell's funerary mitre and staff carved in gilt wood from Christ Church, and a 1586 memorial in oil and wood to Lord Chancellor Thomas More and his wife, Marie, from St. Mary's Church, Adderbury.

Live to Die spoon

Sad to say though, I can't see the Art of Death making a comeback. I mean, imagine commissioning a bust of your little daughter on her deathbed as the parents of Lydia Dwight did in 1674? Or what about stirring your tea for the rest of your natural with the silver mourning spoon the Strickland family commissioned in 1670 to mark the death of a loved one?

'Live to die,' it says on the skull crowned stem – enough to make you wonder whether your other half has slipped a dose of arsenic into your cuppa!

Oxford Mail 18 January 1992

The Gulf War from January 17 to February 28 1991 resulted from Iraq's invasion and annexation of Kuwait in 1990 as a result of an oil dispute. It involved thirty-five nations led by the United States.

Charley's Aunt is a hundred

'It's enough to make a cat laugh,' said the normally strait-laced theatre critic of *The Times* reviewing the first night of *Charley's Aunt* in London on 21 December 1892. A hundred years later it would be hard to find a better expression to describe Walter Brandon Thomas's famous Victorian farce. Hardly a week goes by when there is not a production somewhere in the world.

At one time the play was running simultaneously in forty-eight different theatres in twenty-two different languages including Afrikaans, Chinese, Esperanto, Gaelic, Russian and Zulu.

Audiences who have never set foot in Oxford, let alone heard of undergraduates, talk about 'going down', split their sides at the antics of Lord Fancourt Babberley and his chums, and, strange to say, if they decide to pay the university city a visit on the strength of what they have seen, they find that fiction is not so far from the truth.

Some students still live in attractive oak-panelled rooms with large mullioned windows. In Commemoration Week, if they are lucky, the sunlight does still stream down on manicured college lawns, and college servants are still sometimes good for a loan if your grant runs out!

But why did Liverpudlian Brandon Thomas, born on Christmas Day 1856, choose Oxford for the setting of *Charley's Aunt*, not Cambridge? Mobil Touring Theatre assembled an impressive array of past Charley's Aunts at the home of the Victorian music hall in London, the Players Theatre, to launch their one hundredth birthday production but none of them had asked themselves that question.

It took Janet Birkett of the Theatre Museum in Covent Garden to supply the answer from *Charley's Aunt's Father*, the wittily titled life of Brandon Thomas, which his son Jeavon Brandon-Thomas published in 1956.

When the theatre critic and playwright, Frank Marcus, wrote waspishly of one famous actor's portrayal of Lord Fancourt Babberley in the *Sunday Telegraph* in 1971: 'Tom Courtenay as Charley's Aunt reminded me of Whistler's Mother,' he was nearer the truth than he thought. It was on a visit to Oxford in 1885 to hear *Ten O'clock*, a lecture on art by James

Charley's Aunt: Tom Courtenay chased by Wolfe Morris alias Mr Spettigue
(Punch *cartoon*)

Whistler, the Victorian painter celebrated for his portraits of his mother, that Brandon Thomas fell in love with the university city.

So, when seven years later the noted Victorian comic actor, W.S. Penley, asked him to write a farce for him, Oxford was the setting that sprang to mind. As well as being an ideal location, two features of student life that persisted well into the twentieth century must have appealed to the seasoned actor-playwright's sense of the ridiculous.

One was the convention that well brought up young ladies could not possibly visit a young man's rooms without a chaperone. The other was that because the university authorities regarded actresses as little better than prostitutes, students were forced to dress up in drag for college theatricals.

What better wheeze than one student using his acting weeds to masquerade as a long lost aunt from Brazil so that two of his chums could propose to their sweethearts before they 'went down' from Oxford the next day?

Fearing the London critics might make short work of such a piece of nonsense, Penley tried it out at the Theatre Royal, Bury St. Edmunds, on 29 February 1892. That's why the anniversary production was officially marking the centenary there.

After the first night he sent Brandon Thomas a prophetic telegram: 'Your fortune is assured.' So, to the relief of his creditors queuing up at the stage door was the fortune of the chap who had underwritten the production with £1,000 he didn't possess!

By the time *Charley's Aunt* opened its run of 1,466 performances at the Royalty Theatre, London, in December 1892, the author had taken over the role of Colonel Sir Frank Chesney and he went on to play 'Fanny Babbs' himself in later productions.

The former *Blue Peter* presenter, Mark Curry, who headed the cast of the birthday revival, would be the tenth professional actor to play the part in Oxford since the Second World War.

Donald Hewlett of the *It Ain't Half Hot, Mum* television series did it at the Playhouse in 1951, director Frank Shelley in 1953, Bob Grant from *On the Buses* in 1961; Frankie Howerd, Jimmy Thompson, Julian Holloway and Tom Courtenay at the Apollo Theatre – *now New Theatre again* – in 1956, 1964, 1969, and 1971, and that's just naming the actors who stick in my mind!

Peter Wilson, the director of the one hundredth birthday production, says: 'The secret of *Charley's Aunt's* continuing success is that it is a jolly funny play, much better written than people think,' with a leading role any actor worth his salt can bend to his personality.

'Julian Holloway,' I wrote in the *Oxford Mail* in 1969, 'plays him as a sort of monocled Billy Bunter, who has sloughed off his fat at Oxford but has retained his interest in jolly japes and pranks, his inability to remain out of trouble, and his maniacal laugh.'

As for Whistler's Mother? Reviewing the same production in 1971 I was a bit more downmarket. I said Tom Courtenay is 'a slightly affected young aristocrat who, in moments of stress, becomes a Victorian version of Old

Mother Riley but who never forgets who he is, who the other characters think he is, or the sheer agony of being both of them at once'.

Oxford Mail 27 February 1992

Small change

The new, smaller tenpence piece comes into circulation today – 23 September 1992 — but, before you start moaning about it, count ten! The Royal Mint says it is because we said we wanted smaller, lighter coins they are introducing the new coin – the same reason they gave for introducing the fiddly fivepence piece we all love to hate in June 1990.

Five years ago, the Mint commissioned a team from the University of Nottingham to conduct a survey of the public and those representing special interests like the blind, the elderly, bulk handlers of coinage and the vending industry.

Two messages came over loud and clear: people with sight problems wanted coins with a more pronounced milled edge they could distinguish more easily from other coins. The rest of us, wilting under the weight of heavy handbags, paunchy purses and plummeting pockets, were desperate to lighten the load of money we carried around. The Mint was delighted to oblige. Any excuse they can find to reduce the amount of cupronickel they use to produce the nation's silver has to be good news.

Also making their appearance for the first time are ten billion new one pence and twopence pieces. Unlike the new tenpence piece, they are not the result of a survey. They look the same and feel the same as they always did. Appearances, however, are deceptive. Because the cost of producing them in bronze exceeds their face value, the Mint is making them out of steel with a copper façade.

The Mint has distributed almost 500m of the new tenpence coins to the banks. They are slightly larger but similar in appearance to the old fivepence piece. For the next nine months they will circulate side by side with the old tenpence piece, the coin grandmas and grandpas like to refer to as the two shilling bit or florin.

Then on 30 June 1993 the bigger coin will cease to be legal tender and the process of decimalisation which began in 1971 will at last be complete. Because the Mint thought changing the value of all our coins in one fell swoop would be too much for most of us to handle, they phased it in and the florin is the last survivor of the process.

Tests conducted by a psychologist at Exeter University show that the majority of people who spot a new fivepence piece on the ground cannot be bothered to pick it up and, if the pound goes on sliding, I suppose the new tenpence piece could suffer the same fate.

But provided the banks encourage us to use them, vending machine engineer Paul Rogers of H.R. Vending (Oxford) Ltd, who looks after our coffee and other vending machines at Osney Mead, thinks their introduction should present no mechanical problems. The industry has known they were coming for a long time and most machines should swallow old and new tenpence pieces without suffering indigestion.

Some older machines might cough and splutter over the new coins, just as they might spit out the new twopence and one pence piece, but it's only a matter of making minor adjustments to their innards.

'We've done our work,' says Paul. 'Basically, it's just a matter of getting people to use the new tenpence pieces, and I hope they make a better job of it than they did when they introduced the new fivepence pieces a couple of years ago. That was total chaos. I went into a bank in High Street and asked for some fivepence coins and the cashier tried to fob me off with old ones. "I don't want those," I said, "I want new ones." 'Oh,' she wailed. "You don't really do you? They're down in the cellar."'

Oxford Mail 23 September 1992

16 – Retirement plus

Late in 1993 Eddie Duller said to me: 'Don, if you want to take early retirement, I can fix it for you but you'll have to be quick because I'm going myself.' I needed little encouragement. I had been nursing the idea for a book I wanted to write since 1971. In reality the offer was a reflection of the increasing pressure of a changing world on the newspaper industry. Pearson's could employ two young people for what they paid me.

As it turned out the Oxford Mail ex-deputy editor, David Wynne-Jones, who was now editing the Witney Gazette, begged me to write the West Oxfordshire weekly a regular column and the directors of the Oxford Playhouse commissioned me to write the history of the theatre.

That turned out to involve seven years of research and a part-time doctorate at Leicester University. Hence it was 2011 before I was able to embark on my pet project: working title Angels in Knickers, published by Amberley in 2017 as Wearing the Trousers: Fashion, Freedom and the Rise of the Modern Woman.

As readers of this book will have realised, the Gazette column enabled me to revisit my past to tell quite a few stories that could still bring a smile. It also enabled me to pen one or two more whimsical reflections on the passing scene.

My old china

The other morning, I was scrubbing the cat's plate before giving him his breakfast when it suddenly struck me that that particular piece of chinaware must be at least twenty years old, probably more. The jolly picture of Bopeep looking for her sheep gave the game away. Some kind friend or relation must have given it to one of my daughters when they were learning to feed themselves.

I paused for a minute, wondering how many hundred times I must have recited that nursery rhyme to Katie and Anna as an aid to consumption. Then Pushkar appeared through the catflap, bringing his tail gingerly behind him, rubbed himself against my legs and I stopped daydreaming and reached for the Whiskas.

Domestic crockery is surprisingly durable. Considering most of those clay pots archaeologists dig up come from the favourite hunting grounds of students of the past, the rubbish tip and the pottery reject pile, nothing should survive intact.

Yet how many times, wandering round a museum, have you marvelled at some seemingly pristine piece of tableware, transported yourself back to Ancient Rome, Greece, Egypt or Mesopotamia, and pictured some poor slave doing the washing up?

No? Well, you must have watched one of those experts on popular television antiques programmes waxing lyrical about some priceless teapot or bowl and willed them to drop it!

When we got married my wife, Sue, who is more provident than I am in regard to money matters, deliberately chose a dinner service with a popular pattern so that it would be easy to replace when the inevitable breakages occurred.

Twenty-five years later I am reduced to going one way round car boot sales while she goes the other, hoping against hope that one of us will stumble on a cache of blue-rimmed soup bowls, dinner plates, side plates or pudding dishes.

Yet the bone china Wedgwood tea service a kind friend of Sue's family gave us as a wedding present remains intact. We have lost only one of the fragile Czech glasses with which another relieved friend marked our belated nuptials. And Sue's beloved china cats with the odd chipped ear or broken paw continue to clog my bookshelves.

Given that our kitchen has a quarry tiled floor, it is amazing how many dropped items have bounced. Even the bowl of stew Sue threw at me on one occasion survived unharmed, though the contents did make rather a mess of my shirt.

Only coffee mugs seem to have a short shelf life, and that I suspect is for other reasons. Katie breezes in from Cheltenham, Hereford or whichever hospital she is working in at the moment. Anna pops home from Cambridge, and off they go again after raiding the china cupboard to make good *their* breakages.

Sue prefers the bone china flowered mug I have been taking her not so early morning tea in to her for umpteen years. I don't feel comfortable drinking out of anything other than the handsome earthenware mug embossed with a relief of the SS Great Britain Katie brought back from a trip to Bristol even longer ago.

The truth is that most of us, apart from the accident-prone, of whom I do know a few, have far more crockery than we ever use. In fact, we have far too many possessions altogether.

List the contents of your house, as I hope you do periodically for insurance purposes, then compare it with the contents of the average well-to-do household in the first Elizabethan age. In the days of Elizabeth I, our predecessors managed with a few pewter mugs and plates, a table, some chairs, a fourposter bed if they were lucky, and a chest full of bed linen.

Witney Gazette 10 July 1996

Changing customs

Collecting signatures for the Eynsham and District Liberal Democrat petition opposing the possible deregulation of Swinford Toll Bridge, much against my better judgment we launched our campaign at three o'clock on a Saturday afternoon outside Spar in Eynsham because that was the only time our busy prospective parliamentary candidate could manage.

In the middle of Saturday afternoon, I told myself, most people would be at home with their feet up watching the telly. Not a bit of it. A steady stream came and went from the Spareacre Lane supermarket throughout the two hours we manned our stall.

When I expressed my surprise to our county councillor, Harry Wyatt, he explained: 'Most of them are not shopping for groceries, Don. They're buying their lottery tickets.'

I am not a gambler. As a small boy, a Methodist Sunday school teacher so brainwashed me about the evils of people spending money they could ill afford on horses, dogs, football pools and other forms of betting that to this day I feel guilty forking out tenpence on a raffle ticket.

Consequently, I missed this new departure in the nation's social habits, just as I failed to spot the difference the advent of Sunday trading made to the nation's lifestyle.

It was not until I drove my younger daughter, Anna, into Oxford to catch the coach back to Nottingham and found myself clockwatching anxiously in a long queue of traffic in the Botley Road that I realised going shopping had replaced the post-lunch spin as a Sabbath pastime.

Although an agnostic myself, I have long had a secret admiration for those catholic countries that manage to mix devout religious observances with sin free secular pleasure, attending mass in the morning and a football match in the afternoon, dropping into vespers on the way home from the cinema.

Therefore, I haven't a lot of time for the Keep Sunday

Special brigade. During my time as a junior journalist, I spent too many so-called days of rest fed up and far from home in Keighley to go along with that philosophy.

Make Sunday Special, it has always struck me would be a much better slogan, though sadly now the goings on at the Nine O'clock Service* have come to light even that exhortation is likely to excite knowing sniggers in the ranks of the unbelievers.

The fact is the world moves on and people move with it. We may moan about giving up pounds and ounces for grammes and kilos, abandoning feet and inches for centimetres and metres. We may say we will never get the hang of all those new-fangled weights and measures. Most of us do.

Those traditions that continue to have something to offer our frenetic modern world like morris dancing and Witney Feast survive. Those that don't disappear. Despite the lip service I continue to pay to the excellence of Witney blankets, it's a duvet that keeps me warm at night, as I bet it does most of you.

Take the harvest. Once sheaves of corn and haystacks decorated our stubbled fields at this time of year. Now combine harvesters shoot the grain straight into trailers and leave giant rolls of straw in their wake.

It was with a whoop of delight I opened my *Guardian* the other morning and discovered that in Germany wags

* A church in Sheffield which started a Nine O'clock Service in 1986 to attract younger worshippers had to stop it in 1995 after the Anglican priest running it was accused of hankypanky with some of the girls.

had taken to standing them on end at the edges of fields and decorating them with faces, ties and trousers, bras and aprons. It gives a whole new dimension to the ancient practice of making corn dollies.

Witney Gazette 2 November 1995

And a custom that has resisted change

I always thought the habit of taking a midmorning break dated from the seventeenth century. When Cromwell allowed the Jews back into Britain 350 years after Edward the First had expelled them in 1290, one of the customs they brought with them from the Levant was enjoying a relaxing cup of coffee. Indeed, Jacob the Jew opened the very first coffee house in England at the Angel Inn in High Street, Oxford, a few yards up the road to Carfax from the University Examination Schools.

From that momentous occasion in 1651, I assumed, stemmed the cult we now take for granted: a whole industry, television commercials without number, not to mention reluctant worship punctuated by oaths and scalded fingers at countless coffee machines. It seems not without a struggle.

While doing some research [*for my Playhouse book*] – and incidentally doing without my own elevenses! – in the Bodleian Library, I stumbled on a fascinating passage in a book called *An Oxonian Looks Back* by Lewis R. Farnell.

During his time as Vice-Chancellor of Oxford University from 1920–23, Dr Farnell acquired a reputation for banning everything he didn't fancy from theatrical shows to visiting left-wing politicians.

Among his efforts to 'stiffen up our standard of living' as he put it, was an attempt to put a stop to the midmorning break. 'During the [*First World*] War,' he wrote in his memoirs, 'our overworked officers and men had been in the habit of taking coffee or chocolate or other café stuff when it was possible about eleven in the morning, having frequently been working or fighting since daybreak.' This 'trench habit' they brought home with them, where it spread rapidly in peacetime among the 'well-fed classes'.

Dr Farnell recalled: 'It established itself in Oxford about 1919 or 1920 and our cafés began to do a roaring trade between eleven and twelve in the morning, undergraduates of both sexes sitting there together, indulging themselves with pleasant conversation and unnecessary and unmanly food.'

He decided to put a stop to it by placing the cafés out of bounds to students from ten in the morning to one in the afternoon in much the same way the university already did the bars serving alcoholic refreshments.

One of his proctors, the university officers responsible for policing the undergraduates, supported the ban. The other objected on the grounds that it might put a number of establishments out of business, and would add considerably to the duties of himself and his colleague if they had to go round all the cafés as well as the pubs enforcing it.

That proctor told his wife. She tipped off the women's colleges and 'very soon', Farnell recorded, 'we received an anxious and earnest petition, signed I think by all the lady heads, begging us not to do anything so severe against the poor girls who could not stand the strain of going from nine to one without sustenance. We realised,' he commented with ill-concealed sarcasm, 'a bisexual university had its own special difficulties.'

It was only a few months since the male academics had decided to admit women to full membership, though they would not allow them to take degrees in theology and would continue to limit their numbers until 1956.

Farnell and his henchman felt 'it might be good for the girls' to go without their elevenses. The other proctor dug in his heels. His colleague did not wish to fall out with him. Farnell felt he could hardly insist on a ban they would have to enforce, not him, so he dropped the matter 'to my perpetual regret. For I missed a chance of abolishing a demoralising habit, which I hear now on good authority is injuring Oxford. I wish I had been more ruthless and not so susceptible to the feminine appeal.'

You never know, at the eleventh hour he might have saved us all from the temptation of teabags, the sin of instant coffee, the hell and damnation of hot chocolate. Remember that and thank heaven the next time the refreshment machine gobbles up your money or runs out of change.

Witney Gazette 27 March 1996

The pros and cons of disease

My book at the moment is G.M. Trevelyan's *Shortened History of England*. It has reminded me of something I had forgotten if it ever lodged in my maggoty memory. It was the Black Death that turned us from a nation of ploughmen into a nation of shepherds.

West Oxfordshire owes most of the Cotswold stone churches and manor houses, and Witney its prosperity, to a plague that decimated the population in the fourteenth century. Effectively, the golden fleece of the woollen industry was the chance outcome of a desperate shortage of labour. Fewer hands were needed to tend sheep than to guide ploughs.

Lying abed in the way one does – or at least I do! – half-reading, half-dreaming, it set me wondering what difference other deadly diseases have made to our country. There was, of course, the terrible flu epidemic of 1918. Coming so hard on the carnage and deprivation of the First World War that must have severely hampered Britain's peacetime recovery and another unpleasant disease might easily have affected the outcome of the Second World War.

My dear departed pa-in-law, Professor Gwyn Macfarlane, who told the story of penicillin in two splendid biographies, one of Florey, one of Fleming, was fond of recounting how gonorrhoea caused more casualties in North Africa in 1943 than the enemy.

Penicillin would cure it within twelve hours. The trouble was the new wonder drug was in very short supply. Should the Army doctors use it to save the lives of wounded heroes, or should they squander it on troops laid low as a result of visiting the local brothels?

The dilemma proved so difficult to resolve that eventually Britain's wartime leader, Sir Winston Churchill, was asked to adjudicate. In his famous green ink, he scrawled in the margin of the memo that landed on his desk: 'This valuable drug must on no account be wasted, it must be used to the best military advantage.'

The badly wounded heroes were of no further use to the war effort. The troops with the clap were wanted for the invasion of Sicily. General Poole had no hesitation in telling Florey to treat them – on the orders of the Prime Minister!

I suppose it was too early in the nineteen-nineties to say what long term impact AIDS, the most dreadful scourge of the twentieth century would have on the future, but it affected our lives profoundly. Except among preachers of hellfire and damnation, who regarded it as a punishment from God for unnatural practices, I think it led to a greater understanding of and sympathy for the gay community. What is more, it resulted in the open promotion of safe sex, a subject most of our grandparents and great-grand-parents would have died to think might one day feature in Government sponsored television commercials.

I myself suffer from a less life-threatening affliction that has also hit the headlines in recent years: myalgic encephalomyelitis, ME or, as it is now often called chronic fatigue syndrome or, less kindly, 'yuppy flu'. Some experts believe it has been around for centuries.

The eminent medical historian, my good friend Dr

Alastair Robb-Smith of Woodstock, once told me, half joking, half serious, he reckoned the Elizabethan and Jacobean melancholy poets all suffered from it. That's why their poems were so gloomy!

Now *Perspectives*, the magazine of the Myalgic Encephalomyelitis Association, has published an article by Sandra Howes claiming the first known description of a disease resembling ME occurred in a fragment of Egyptian papyrus written nearly 4,000 years ago. A later victim may have been Ann Boleyn, who picked up something very similar called the English Sweat Henry VIII's army brought back from a campaign in Holland.

Should I be glad or sorry Florence Nightingale might have suffered for twenty-five years in the nineteenth century from the same trouble as has affected me for the last ten? Well, I suppose you could say that I'm in good company.

Witney Gazette 15 November 1995

Easter wrapped up

My ma-in-law, Witney's first woman GP, Dr Hilary Macfarlane, gives up chocolate for Lent. A real sacrifice. There is nothing she enjoys more after her lunch or evening meal than a square of plain chocolate, an After Eight, or a Black Magic soft centre. So, on Easter Sunday it has become a tradition over the years for my wife, Sue, to mark the end of her mum's self-imposed fast by presenting her with a large chocolate egg.

Living as she did until recently at the top of Scotland, it took a bit of organising. Sue would arrange for Duncan, the proprietor of the nearest shop, to obtain and wrap the gift. She would dispatch a cheque, and on Easter Saturday it would make the four-mile journey from Laide to Opinan with the milk or the post.

For several weeks it would sit in pristine elegance on the sideboard at the croft in Wester Ross my ma-in-law retired to seventeen years ago with her late husband. Then at last she would summon up the courage to break into it and my wife would receive a delighted telephone call from her saying: 'Guess what I'm doing. I'm eating your delicious egg!'

This Easter there was no cause to ring Duncan. Failing eyesight has forced my ma-in-law to give up her beloved home in the West Highlands and move south to a more convenient house round the corner from us in Eynsham. But the tradition of the chocolate egg continues and for a few days the latest edition sat on the same sideboard in West Oxfordshire.

Then, I suppose, realism getting the better of sentiment, ma-in-law decided there wasn't much point pretending to appreciate the appearance of an egg she couldn't really see and broke into it. With my occasional scribblings for the *Witney Gazette* in mind, she described the experience for me blow by blow.

'First, I took it out of its box. Wrapper No. One. Then I released it from its casing. Wrapper No. Two. Then I lifted it out of its plastic container. Wrapper No. Three. Then I took off the silver paper. Wrapper No. Four. Inside the big egg was a cellophane bag containing a number of little eggs. Wrapper No. Five. I opened that and popped a baby egg into my mouth and what do you think? Wrapper No. Six! Dash it, that was covered in silver paper too!'

My dear ma-in-law doesn't like to speculate how much her daughter paid for her chocolate egg and how much for the six wrappers she had to fight her way through in order to start eating it. But if lesser creatures can manage with one to maintain the reproductive cycle, it does seem sad that Easter Egg manufacturers have to litter the planet with six to protect a few ounces of chocolate.

I use the word litter advisedly. Stuffed in the hedgerow a couple of days later on our morning walk Sue and I spotted the remains of a child's Easter chocolate treat. Box, casing, plastic container, silver paper, the lot!

Witney Gazette 11 May 1995

Growing old disgracefully

When she was four, my mother spent a day walking across the green fields of London with her twin sister and elder brother to see their first aeroplane and another two days recovering after they got back. Sixty years later my daughters took their first look at Mars without stirring from the living room.

In another ten my grandchildren will probably be playing digitally with their cousins on the other side of the world. It's already happening. Not long ago my brother-in-law, Jay Macfarlane, who emigrated to Australia more than twenty-five years ago, arrived from Perth bearing an electronic notebook no bigger than a two-pound box of chocolates.

It not only enabled him to keep tabs on his laser-cutting business down under while he was visiting his mum in Eynsham. It meant he could continue to share the odd game of cards with his workforce during their lunch hour. 'Rather a frivolous way to run up a telephone bill,' I commented. 'Not at all, Don,' he grinned. 'The computer shuffles and deals the pack in under a second.'

Every time I shop at my village supermarkets, I marvel at the electronic cash tills at the checkout counters. Provided I've remembered to bring my glasses, I can read every item I've bought, what I've paid for it, how much I gave the cashiers and what change they gave me, all neatly printed out on a receipt while I'm still fumbling to open my carrier bag.

Clearly tomorrow's world will be wonderful if my definition of progress – running hard to stay in the same place – remains as true for my children and grandchildren as it has been for my parents and me.

Nonetheless, I'm afraid the twenty-first century is going to be just as traumatic as the twentieth. The motorcar increases our mobility and punches holes in the ozone layer. Healthier living makes us last longer and cripples the National Health Service with demands for triple bypasses and hip replacements.

It's all very well for Bob Hoskins to flit about in the BT

television commercials like a fat fairy plugging the benefits of keeping in touch. But can you imagine what it will be like when people can contact you by videophone?

What will you tell the double-glazing salesman when he can see you haven't got the latest triple-plated safety windows, let alone a shiny new plastic, suction-sealed, multi-locking front door? How will you cope with opinion pollsters who pursue you into the loo to ask you if you'd mind putting down your crossword for a moment to tell MORI why you prefer Harpic to Sanilav? Where will you be able to hide beyond the reach of well-meaning loved ones on days when you don't feel like shaving or doing the washing up?

As my old brainbox, the personal commuter that has served me so well for a long lifetime begins to malfunction, I reserve the right to grow old disgracefully. I'm not sure I want to see my name down on a John Radcliffe Hospital waiting list for a new microchip.

Personal Column *Witney Gazette* 20 October 1994

Acknowledgements

I have been lucky with my book editors. Jane Housham and Sarah Elvins of the University of Hertfordshire Press did a sterling job on *Oxford Playhouse: High and low drama in a university city*. Cathy Stagg, ex-general history editor of Amberley Publishing was equally enthusiastic and sympathetic in her handling of my history of rational dress, *Wearing the Trousers: Fashion, Freedom and the Rise of the Modern Woman*. Now I have James Essinger and his team at The Conrad Press to thank for publishing my latest book: James himself for his enthusiasm for and masterminding into print of *A Tenpenny Dip in Paradise and other flights of fancy*, and the husband-and-wife team who run The Book Typesetters for the look of my book: Nat Ravenlock for the crisp typescript, Rachael for the fantastic cover.

I have personal reasons to feel proud to join The Conrad Press stable of authors. My wife Sue's father's mother was one of the Sanderson children who befriended Joseph Conrad when he abandoned his maritime career because of ill health in 1893. It was in their house he wrote his first novel, *Almayer's Folly*, and to their mother, Sue's great grandmother, Katherine Sanderson, he dedicated *The*

308

Mirror of the Sea, his first book of 'memories and impressions', saying her warm welcome and gracious hospitality cheered the first dark days of his parting with the sea. Our elder daughter Katherine takes her name from her.

Inevitably most of the people who feature in my own tongue in cheek memories and impressions are dead, but hopefully some of them come alive again in its pages. Of those who do not, I should mention Fred Page, a sub-editor on the Bradford *Telegraph and Argus*, who initiated a series of inspiring training sessions for junior journalists, and Raynor Chapman (no relation), one of the Westminster Press's most senior editors, who luckily for me edited the *Keighley News* during the eighteen months I was there between more senior appointments. He first encouraged me to spread my wings and when I left paid me the ambivalent compliment: 'Don, you may never be as good a day-to-day reporter as those who use words like nuts and bolts, you care too much about what you write, but you have the makings of a fine journalist.'

Of the colleagues I worked with in Oxford several went on to make their names in what was then Fleet Street, to edit national and regional papers or play influential roles in radio and television. I stayed put to be greeted fondly by them when they popped back to Oxford, envied for my more relaxed, less frenetic lifestyle, my ability to keep my finger on the pulse of the local community, my life in the country, and my unfailing relish for expressing a droll sense of humour in print.

In gathering this selection of articles, I am greatly indebted to my former colleague, ex-news editor John

Chipperfield, who found several photographs and other material in the now sadly truncated *Oxford Mail and Times* library for me and to the staff of the Oxfordshire History Centre for locating other stories I recalled writing but had no cuttings for. Especially I would like to thank Keighley Local Studies customer support assistant Gina Birdsall at Keighley Library for tracking down the history of the public baths, from which my book takes its title.

A Tenpenny Dip in Paradise and other flights of fancy is dedicated to my wife Sue, who shared my journey, reined in my wilder excesses, provided a number of the more striking illustrations and proof-read and occasionally improved the readability of my writing. Although I give the dates when the articles first appeared in print, I have not hesitated to tweak them where necessary and apologise in advance for any shortcomings, errors and omissions.

May 2022